SHINE

24 Successful Business Leaders Share How They Inspire Themselves And Others To Go For It And Grow!

Edited By Joan Scott & Andrew Priestley

WM

SHINE

Edited By Joan Scott and Andrew Priestley

First published in May 2025

W&M Publishing

ISBN 978-1-917265-47-8 Pbk

The rights of Joan Scott and Andrew Priestley (Editors) and Jamie Edwards (Foreword), Sue Belton, Joan Scott, Kylie Denton, Candice Gardner, Jacqui Lee, Fiona Jackson, Arif Isikgun, Andrea Simpson, Joanne Serrant, Kath Reade, Kay Pennington, Lucy Power, Susanne Webb, Fabienne Guichon Lindholm, Melissa Timperley, Jacqueline O'Sullivan, Diane Hey, Madeleine Geach, Anne Taylor, Jaimie Sarah, Louise Baker, Andrew Priestley and Jen Buck to be identified as contributing authors of this work has been asserted in accordance with Sections 77 and 78 of the Copyright Designs and Patents Act, 1988.

A CIP catalogue record for this book is available from the British Library.

Disclaimer: Shine is intended for information and education purposes only. This book does not constitute specific legal, financial, health, clinical or commercial advice unique to your situation.

The views and opinions expressed in this book are those of the author and do not reflect those of the Publisher and Resellers, who accept no responsibility for loss, damage or injury to persons or their belongings as a direct or indirect result of reading this book.

All people mentioned in case studies have been used with permission, or details altered to protect client confidentiality. Any similarity to actual persons, living or dead, or actual events, is purely coincidental.

Marianne Williamson's (2015) *Our Deepest Fear* from *A Return To Love: A Return to Love: Reflections on the Principles of a Course in Miracles*, Harper Thorsons is reprinted with kind permission.

Contents

Foreword: Your World Needs You To Shine

Jamie Edwards

There's a saying I often use in my work:

A candle doesn't discover who it really is in the light.

It only finds its true strength and identity in the dark.

When Joan Scott first approached me to write a chapter for this book, time didn't allow me to do that fully.

But there was no way I was going to miss the opportunity to be part of a project called Shine.

Because helping people shine — not just when it's easy, but when it's hard — is at the very core of my life's work.

Over the last two decades, I have been blessed to guide people in some of the most unforgiving worlds imaginable from the cutthroat world of professional sports...

...to the high-stakes pressure of business leadership,

...to walk alongside women facing the fight of their lives against cancer.

Across all these arenas, I have seen the same truth play out again and again:

We don't find out who we are when everything is going well.

We find out who we are when it gets dark.

Nobody comes because life is perfect.

Nobody looks for expansion when everything feels easy.

True resilience, true leadership, true courage — they are all forged when the lights go out, when the easy answers aren't there, and when the only thing you have left to trust... is the flame inside you.

That is what Shine represents.

Each chapter in this book is a story of someone who found themselves not because the world handed them the perfect conditions — but because they learned to light their own way through the challenges.

In my work at *TrainedBrain*, we talk about mastering the *Four Quadrants* of your life: *Body, Being, Inner Circle,* and *Business.*

Succeeding in one area isn't enough.

Real success — lasting success — happens when you commit to shining your light in every domain, even when the darkness tries to convince you to give up.

As you move through these pages, I encourage you to listen for the light inside each story — the moment where a leader, a person, a human being — had to meet themselves honestly at the crossroads.

Not the moment they got the medal, but the moment they wondered if they could take another step.

And ask yourself:

- Where is the darkness in my life asking me to rise, not retreat?
- Where is my next evolution being forged, not because everything is perfect, but because I am willing to keep my flame alive?

The pit moments — the hard seasons — are not signs that you're failing.

They are the places where your true light gets activated.

So many people believe they need better conditions to shine.

But the truth is: you don't need a different set of circumstances.

You need a different relationship with the circumstances you're in.

Reading Shine won't change your life on its own.

But if you let it, if you let it touch your heart and your hunger, it can provoke the most important questions you will ever ask yourself — and provoke the courage you already have inside you to answer them.

I want to leave you with this:

You are the light you've been waiting for.

You are the leader you've been hoping to meet.

You are closer than you think.

And the world — your world — needs you to Shine.

Especially when it's dark.

Here's to the light inside you.

Here's to your next chapter.

Jamie Edwards

Jamie Edwards is one of the world's leading mental performance coaches, called upon when the lights are going out — or have already gone out. He has guided Premiership and Champions League winners, Ashes and Ryder Cup heroes, MDs, founders, and their leadership teams at pivotal moments of their careers and lives. His holistic TrainedBrain approach is trusted by organisations committed to sustainable impact. Jamie's passion is giving people the tools before they think they need them — helping them meet, not just reach, their potential by finding the light within and learning to shine outwardly again.

www.trained-brain.com

jedwards@trained-brain.com

You Are Welcome To SHINE

"Don't die with your music still inside you"
Dr. Wayne Dyer

Do you have a yearning to do something? It could be a new role, a bid for a project, developing a new business, submitting a nomination for an award, entering a competition or finally booking that trip of a lifetime. It doesn't matter what it is, it could be a dream job or a long-held goal – but, what's stopping you? Are you over-thinking the downsides? The 'what if …..? What if I don't get the job? What if I don't deliver a successful project? What if the business fails? What if I don't win the competition or the award? What if I don't enjoy the trip?

BUT... *what if you do?*

The only failure is not trying. You're going to fail at 100% of the things you don't try.

What's your dream? What would you do if you knew you couldn't fail?

I love the quote from Tim Grover. *'If you think the price of winning is too high, wait until you get the bill for regret.'* The words hit you hard and force you to face what you're putting off, what you're delaying or finding excuses for.

When you reflect….

What do you want to do?

Who do you want to be?

Where do you want to go?

With whom?

When?

So... what's stopping you?

We may be putting things off until the perfect time arrives, or the perfect scenario is in place. Constantly finding reasons why now isn't the time to move forward with these hopes and dreams. If only we realised there will never be a perfect time, it doesn't exist. We also think we have all the time in the world.

Confucius said, 'We all have two lives; the second one starts when we realise we only have one.'

What are we worried about? That we'll fail and lose face for trying? I believe there are no downsides: you either succeed or you learn from the experience. It's a win-win.

Nelson Mandela summed it up perfectly. 'I never lose. Either I win or learn.' With such a mindset, every day is a school day, we learn continually, and we grow consistently as a result.

The big question is- how do we motivate ourselves or encourage others to go for it, to take the first step, to embrace the opportunity, to cherish the challenge, to take action, however small.

That's often all it takes... one simple step. Lao Tzu said, *'The journey of a thousand miles begins with one step'* and indeed it does. Once you take the first few steps, you gain confidence and skills, and create the momentum to continue.

'You don't have to see the whole staircase, just take the first step' is a quote by Martin Luther King Jr that underlines this approach. You've got to develop a mindset that reinforces the view that you'll never lose if you take action and simply move forward.

To begin, you will need to look at your motivation – what is driving you? What do you want to achieve or experience? Many call this your 'Why?' Once you establish *why* you want to do something, and what you are doing this for, this can act like a compass. When the journey gets challenging it can draw you back to your main direction, your 'north star'.

But is it motivation you need? Or is it just a commitment, and then the discipline to be consistent?

If you establish a habit and the discipline to practice these habits frequently, many believe this is better than trying to find the elusive motivation. Motivation can get you started, but it is consistency of action that leads to progress and ultimately achieves success. Procrastination can be challenging; many suffer from the desire to avoid what they should be doing – sometimes this can be linked to perfectionism- they don't want to start if they feel they can't do the task perfectly.

Once you have started, you will need courage to keep going and move from your comfort zone into the unknown.

It can be frightening as you're pushing yourself in a direction that you haven't experienced before — there could be lots of excitement, but also some fear. Therefore it's important to continually remember your 'why'- your reason for doing all this.

There will be bumps in the road, maybe diversions and roadblocks, but embrace them all, as there is learning in each of them. You can learn more from a challenging journey than from a smooth, uneventful trip. Success can be achieved on the 10th time of doing something, don't give up on the 9th try. The result you want might be just around the corner.

George M Moore summed it up by saying, 'A winner is just a loser who tried one more time.'

This approach is demonstrated by Thomas Edison, he made thousands of attempts before he finally found the right filament to create the electric light bulb.

Courage to keep trying and persistence to keep going pays off. Susan Jeffers encourages us all to 'Feel the fear and do it anyway.' Acknowledge there may be times you feel fearful and anxious, but embrace it. Use it to fuel your action.

Once you've decided to go for it, and are consistently practising the habits, you will develop new skills and more confidence in your own ability — which in turn will spur you on even more.

This self-belief and self-respect will serve you well, in all aspects of your life. You can have belief in yourself when maybe others don't. But you know deep down what you are capable of, and you're going to prove it.

With more confidence you will lean in to situations as opposed to using avoidance techniques. The positive feedback you receive will empower you to go further.

If you embrace lots of situations, and some don't go according to plan, you will learn so much, and you will undoubtedly develop more resilience. Things might not actually get easier, but they feel easier as you will be more experienced and stronger, with lots more skills and techniques and a mindset that embraces change and setbacks. You may find that in the middle of challenging times you find the diamond in the dust – which could be an opportunity you hadn't even considered.

Resilience can be likened to a muscle – you have to use it, or you lose it. Tackling challenges allows us to tap into skills and strengths we never knew we had, we often surprise ourselves. This in turn develops more confidence and an ability to lean even further into situations.

We can't talk about stepping into new opportunities and delivering excellence without mentioning hard work. Many will say there is no substitute for hard work.

Maya Angelou said, *'Nothing will work unless you do'* underling the fact you need to take action and make great effort in the direction of your goals.

Some individuals are blessed with natural talent, and it can seem unfair to have to compete with these people, do you stand a chance? However, some naturally talented individuals don't have a strong work ethic, and the term *'Hard work beats talent when talent doesn't work hard'* was a quote that inspired NBA superstar Kevin Durant and helped him achieve his goals.

All the different aspects I've previously mentioned are the cornerstones of a flexible growth mindset, as opposed to a fixed mindset. A winning mindset is definitely a growth mindset. People with this approach are willing to get uncomfortable, to fully focus on their goal, and they are very intentional and courageous.

Carol Dwek developed the *growth mindset* model. From all her extensive research she found that *'The passion for stretching yourself and sticking to it, even (or especially) when it's not going well, is the hallmark of the growth mindset. This is the mindset that allows people to thrive during some of the most challenging times in their lives.'*

We hear that many young people are focussed on perfectionism. This may be the result of the influence of social media, with everyone showcasing a perfect image and a perfect lifestyle. A recent poll found that Gen Z feel pressure to only be perfect...immediately...increasednegative emotions like anxiety.

Approximately one in three Gen Zers struggle with perfectionism. This desire to be perfect, can result in a reluctance to try different things and can often prevent them from starting a task, or challenging themselves, as they fear failure. They can never meet these unachievable goals, which can have a detrimental effect on their mental health and wellbeing. This *fixed mindset,* can result in many missed opportunities. They miss out personally, but also, we all miss out, as they are less likely to realise their full potential in the family, in the workplace and in life generally. If we can help them to develop a more flexible mindset, it could be transformational.

I'm excited for you to meet the SHINE authors, they share their personal story about embracing a growth mindset. Many have challenged themselves to step out of their comfort zone and follow a dream or goal. Others have worked with their team, their students or their mentees. All have provided inspiration and a framework to support themselves and others to develop a growth mindset, so they can fulfil their true potential.

Life moves so quickly, please embrace all your opportunities and find inspiration in these stories, so you can continue to shine, and in turn light the way for others.

Joan Scott (Editor)

The Drivers That Dimmed Me (And How I Reclaimed My Light)

Sue Belton

To shine – what does that even mean?

Or maybe the better question is: to what degree are you *not* shining?

Because let's be honest, that's what most of us are doing – dimming ourselves, holding back, not being who we fully are. We shrink to fit. We downplay the very things that make us unique. We pile layer upon layer over the parts of ourselves that are raw, radiant, real.

And I include myself in this. Fully.

For most of my adult life, I was someone who, from the outside, looked like I had it all sorted. Confident. High-achieving. Driven. Had an opinion on everything. Definitely someone you'd call "successful."

But underneath? I was constantly afraid.

Afraid I'd be found out. Afraid I didn't really belong. Afraid that unless I kept achieving, striving, working harder, playing harder, I'd lose whatever worth I'd managed to prove. That without the next goal, the next shiny thing, I was... nothing. I didn't add up to much.

My life didn't add up to much.

That fear didn't come from nowhere. It had roots. Like most of us, my childhood shaped the lens through which I saw myself and the world.

As a child, often I didn't feel seen. I didn't feel anyone got me. My creativity? My sensitivity? My hunger to be understood and appreciated? It wasn't really celebrated. And on top of that, I was an "army brat". We moved every couple of years, mostly around Germany, until I was ten and we landed permanently in England. Which meant no lasting friendships, no roots. Always the new kid.

Moving to England was a shock. Suddenly, I was this weird outsider, dropped into a school on a housing estate in Grantham – a small, grey market town in Lincolnshire (yes, birthplace of both Isaac Newton and Margaret Thatcher). I got labelled 'Nazi' by the other kids. Didn't matter that I was British. The accent, the difference, was enough.

Eventually, I was moved to another school in town. The kids were more open-minded, or at least less cruel. That's when I discovered drama – playing Jesus, playing Nora Batty (yes, really) – and for the first time, I felt something like belonging.

Then came a big turning point: passing the eleven-plus and getting into Kesteven and Grantham Girls' School. That place saved me. I found my people – other girls who were quirky, different, bright, curious. I wasn't 'too much' for them. I wasn't weird. I was home.

I'm still close to two of those girls – now women – Ashley and Lucy. At 53, that kind of friendship is gold.

What I didn't realise until much later was how much that school shaped me in another way. It gave me a glimpse of what life could be like without gender being a barrier. I didn't think being a woman made life harder – until I entered the workplace.

That's when reality hit. Sexual harassment. Being told I was 'too ambitious' (in that tone that turns something powerful into something problematic). Suddenly, there were rules I hadn't signed up for. And old fears started creeping back.

I'm not sharing all this for sympathy. I'm sharing it because these are the things that get in the way of us shining.

And because what I've come to see – personally, professionally, and in working with countless others – is that we all develop patterns early on. Ways of being. Coping strategies. And while they help us survive as kids, they often hold us hostage as adults.

For me, it showed up like this:

- The need to get everything right all the time. Waking at 4am in a panic about something I may have said or done wrong.

- The need to cope no matter what. To be the strong one. Never ask for help, never accept it. God forbid someone might think I can't handle things.

- The need to get everything done immediately. If something's on my list, it has to be finished now. And of course, there's always another thing right behind it.

- The need to be busy. Always. Because space in the diary makes me feel lazy, or worse – worthless.

These needs aren't personality quirks. They're what psychologists call drivers – unconscious patterns we adopt early to fit in, feel safe, and be loved.

And let's be really clear: they block our shine.

They stop us from doing what we truly want. They kill joy. They kill creativity. They stop us from showing up fully in our relationships and work. They stopped me from speaking in public without panic, from going for big dreams (hello, childhood Blue Peter presenter fantasy), from truly collaborating. And yep – loneliness was a symptom too.

They even stopped me from resting. From enjoying life. From being present.

Any of this sounding familiar?

If so, you're not broken. You're human.

The drive behind all of this is the deep, primal need to feel OK. To be worthy. To be loved. And somewhere along the way, we started believing that we had to earn that love. That we weren't enough just being ourselves.

But here's the truth: you are.

And until we start to untangle those early survival patterns, we'll keep dimming ourselves to fit in. We'll keep playing small.

So, what are these drivers? There are five key ones, and most of us have at least two – sometimes all five in different degrees.

The Five Drivers

1. **Be Perfect** – You have to get everything 100% right. Mistakes are terrifying. Flaws feel fatal.

2. **Be Strong** – You're the responsible one. You don't need help. You hold it all together – always.

3. **Try Hard** – Effort is everything. You've got to push, push, push. Hustle. Strive. Never ease up.

4. **Hurry Up** – Time is running out. Everything has to happen now. Resting is lazy. Pausing is dangerous.

5. **Please Others** – Other people's needs come first. You shape-shift, accommodate, overextend – because that's how you feel valued.

Ring any bells?

These patterns are sneaky. They sound like virtues. Our culture even praises them. But they're insidious. They keep us locked in habits that drain our energy and dull our light.

So how do we begin to break free?

We start with awareness.

And then we counter each driver with its antidote – what's called an *'Allower Statement.'*. These are simple, powerful truths that start to rewire the script.

The Allowers

1. **Be Perfect** > You're good enough exactly as you are.

2. **Be Strong** > It's safe to ask for help.

3. **Try Hard** > You don't have to push to be worthy.

4. **Hurry Up** > Take it steady. You have time.

5. **Please Others** > Your wants and needs matter too.

These aren't affirmations to stick on a post-it and forget. These are rewrites for your nervous system. They're daily practices. Lifelines. Invitations back to your real self.

And when you start to live from this place – more honest, less driven by fear – you don't just change your life. You give permission to others. Your light helps others find theirs.

I learned that on my coach training, seventeen years ago, when I was asked to read a poem aloud to a group of eighteen people. I broke down crying halfway through. Not because I was sad, but because it cracked something open in me. Maybe it will for you too.

Our Deepest Fear

Marianne Williamson

Our deepest fear is not that we are inadequate.

Our deepest fear is that we are powerful beyond measure.

It is our Light, not our Darkness, that most frightens us.

We ask ourselves, who am I to be brilliant, gorgeous,
talented, fabulous?

Actually, who are you not to be?

You are a child of God.
Your playing small does not serve the world.

There is nothing enlightened about shrinking

so that other people won't feel insecure around you.

We were born to make manifest the glory of God
that is within us.

It's not just in some of us; it is in everyone.

And as we let our own light shine, we unconsciously
give other people permission to do the same.

As we are liberated from our own fear,
our presence automatically liberates others.

This is what it means to *shine*.

Not perfection. Not constant effort. Not people-pleasing.
But honesty. Courage. Aliveness.

You get to be you. Fully. Messily. Brilliantly.

And that – that – is how we change the world.

Williamson. M. (2015) Our Deepest Fear from A Return To Love: A Return to Love: Reflections on the Principles of a Course in Miracles, Harper Thorsons. Used with kind permission

And here's the thing – I'm not just talking about this stuff anymore. I'm living it.

I'm still a work-in-progress (aren't we all?), but I've been actively challenging and shifting those old driver behaviours. Bit by bit, breath by breath.

Yes, I now regularly stand up and speak in front of groups. I still get a bit nervous, sure – but I no longer panic. I remind myself I'm OK. I know my stuff. And even if I don't know everything? That's OK too.

I'm much better at sharing responsibility now – letting others take the reins, allowing myself to be supported. That one still pokes at my edges from time to time, but I'm working on it.

I've slowed down. A lot. I rest. I take breaks. I 'smell the roses' more than I ever used to. And when I catch myself speeding up again – because old habits die hard – I breathe, pause, and reset.

I'm proud to say I've become very good at doing 'nothing.' Sitting in the garden, watching the birds. Lying in bed in the morning with a coffee, chatting away with my fiancé Andrew. And I don't feel guilty about the holidays we take on a regular basis. In fact, I soak them up.

Because this is what shining looks like for me now: ease, connection, enough-ness, presence.

And if I can reclaim that light – so can you.

About Sue Belton

Sue Belton is an award-winning leadership coach who helps high-achieving leaders reconnect with what truly matters – so they can lead with impact, confidence, and authenticity.

She specialises in working with successful SME Founders, Senior Leaders, and C-Level Executives who are ready to step out of overdrive and into the kind of leadership that shines from the inside out.

Based in London, her global client base includes names like Getty Images, Virgin Wines, Curtis Brown, and Generali.

Named Female Entrepreneur of the Year and Best Coach, Sue was also a finalist in the Business Book Awards for her bestselling debut Change Your Life in 5. And follow-up, Screw Meditation! Her podcast Change Makers: Ordinary People Making Extraordinary Changes has reached audiences in 28 countries.

Known for getting real, going deep, and creating lasting change, Sue believes that when leaders stop running on autopilot and start showing up as their whole selves, everyone benefits – teams thrive, clients stay loyal, and businesses grow.

Because when leaders shine, everyone around them rises too.

www.suebelton.com

A Chance To Shine

Joan Scott

'What would you do if you weren't afraid?"
Sheryl Sandberg

This book was almost called, *'You win, or you learn.'* Simple. To the point. Exactly my thinking at the time.

Then when I really thought about it, I realised it was far more complex than that. I didn't want it to be a compete at all costs approach. But more of a way to look at how you live your life- how you make the most of your opportunities, how you work hard and keep learning, how you grow and develop resilience and ultimately how you follow your hopes, dream and goals. Ultimately, it is a book about developing a *Growth Mindset* and not being afraid to shine.

In my role, I'm lucky to work with so many wonderful educators. One of my aims is to inspire them to see how amazing skills competitions are. How they can enrich and enhance their curriculum delivery, and how they can provide wonderful opportunities for their learners. It is my hope that the educators will inspire and motivate their students to see the many benefits of participating, and in turn they decide to wholly embrace competition opportunities. By doing this, the young people, and adults, will increase their technical and employability skills, and enhance their curriculum vitae (CV) and personal statements, which are a key part of their application for employment and for university.

Developing this type of mindset is equally as valuable if you're leading a team, or influencing family members to work hard, learn continually and build resilience. Those with this approach to life tend to achieve more than those who have a more fixed mindset. This fixed approach suggests talents are what you are born with and life either gives you certain gifts, or it doesn't. To help others shine must be one of the most valuable things you can do for another person.

'What if I fall? ......but oh darling, what if you fly?'
Erin Hanson

Many young people arrive in further education (FE) lacking confidence, without a career focus or a great work ethic. A high number of them have never been told they're good at anything. This is so sad, and it can have many consequences. Very often they've never had any positive feedback from school or their family, as a result they're not sure which course is ideal for their career goals, and they've not developed any ambitions.

Building skills competitions into the curriculum has been a great approach for many years, but it is now gaining further momentum as more benefits are recognised. The feedback provided from short classroom competitions can really motivate a learner. It might be the first positive feedback they've had about the skills they possess. It can help inspire them to do more, go further, gain confidence and grow in many ways, both personally and professionally. As an educator, it's so rewarding to witness this change.

In my career as a leader, I look back and realise that I used the phrase, *'It's a chance to shine'* many times. It was my go-to phrase when I was encouraging and persuading members of the team to stretch themselves, such as when there were opportunities to get involved in a project, a VIP visit, a presentation or a promotion. I would always 'sell' the opportunity rather than 'tell' it, explaining the potential benefits if they embraced it, and how they would grow. I always explained that you never know what you will learn, who you will meet, or what it could lead to.

My personal view is that you must trust the process, and see what life has in store for you. Sometimes it surprises you with opportunities beyond your wildest dreams. Embracing a challenge could lead to somewhere amazing; it's not simply luck, it often involves hard work, grit and determination. I love the quote, *'Hard work puts you where good luck can find you.'*

Another phase I fully resonate with is, *'Its only when you look back that you see how the dots were joined up all along'.* At the time you never know where it's all leading, or the importance of certain events or opportunities. I think I was 8 or 9 years old when I developed a love of competitions. I now wonder if it was because I was very shy and lacking in confidence, and I found that competitions rewarded you for trying your absolute best. Competition success was quite addictive, your confidence soars as you gain recognition that your work is good and is being celebrated. At junior school I was good at art, and won a farm safety poster competition, which I'll never forget. My competitive streak led me to becoming a bit of a Blue Peter badge groupie, getting two traditional ones, a silver one and even stalking the BBC to ask how I could get a gold one. Apparently, these were only awarded to children who had saved someone from drowning or rescued people from a house fire and I'm sad to say I was plotting how I could do something similar!

> 'Competition ignites passion, determination,
> and the pursuit of excellence.'
> Serena Williams

When I was studying at college, I had the opportunity to enter competitions, and in my final year I won the major trophy, sponsored by Colgate-Palmolive. Again, this is something I've never ever forgotten. It made me feel proud, and increased my confidence knowing the standard of my work was very high and had been recognised. Looking back, I think I sought out these opportunities because I was lacking in confidence, I was insecure, and I felt out of my depth in the big city after moving from a small village in Cumbria. I know how much participating in these competitions helped me personally, and that's why I want as many young people as possible to have similar experiences. School might have been a negative experience for them, family members perhaps don't recognise they have any positive skills, knowledge or behaviours. Very often these youngsters thrive in a college environment, they find a welcoming place where they can study a subject they love, plus they get feedback that they do have many talents.

This can be a transformational time in their life.

The curriculum itself gives ample opportunities to develop great technical skills, and the wider, personal life skills that employers are looking for. My view is that the qualification should be the least they leave college with. Great teachers are always looking to enrich and enhance the course in a variety of ways, such as the involvement of employers from industry providing masterclasses and career insights. The opportunity to get involved in skill competitions is another chance to enrich the course, it can be a key part of the curriculum delivery. This could include internal classroom competitions, inter-college competitions, or regional and national opportunities such as those offered by WorldSkills UK.

Throughout my career I've always tried to embrace every opportunity that came my way. This included working in a physiotherapy practice, having my own business, teaching, being a manager, an examiner, a judge, applying for promotion, doing an MSc, being an author, ...it was never easy, but always so interesting, so immensely rewarding and it has given me an amazing, fulfilling career.

Not everything went well, sometimes I didn't achieve what I set out to accomplish, but I developed a way of embracing the outcome no matter what.

As I get older and perhaps a little wiser and more spiritual, I always frame a disappointment with the thought, *I wonder what's coming my way that's even better than what I was aiming for?*.

My spirituality has been known to go a little woo-woo (..or a lot) and I'm convinced the saying 'the universe has your back' is right. Everything seems to work out in the end, there's no point worrying unnecessarily, the best approach is to hope for the best, prepare for the worst, celebrate everything.

When I was a teacher, I always encouraged students to get involved in skills competitions and other opportunities to grow, so they embraced all the chances open to them, and did their best. My approach was that you'll either win, get placed or learn so much that you grow and improve, and are ready for the next time. They would develop personally and professionally; I encouraged them to focus less on the outcome and more on the process of learning from each competitive experience. After all, it was a chance to shine, and we need to embrace each opportunity.

I'm proud to coordinate the Greater Manchester Colleges Skills Competitions. They involve more than 1,000 learners taking part in over 70 individual competitions, from digital and engineering, to enterprise and construction. It's such a great opportunity for young people and all nine colleges work together to encourage educators to motivate their learners to get involved. This can add variety to curriculum delivery, increase challenge, and be a fun way to learn. It can simulate the work place as there is often pressure to perform to a high standard in a limited time period. It's my view that excellent teaching, learning and assessment encompasses skills competitions. They are not simply an add-on, it's more fundamental than that. Inspectors of education are often looking for exceptionality – to go above and beyond, to stretch and challenge learners helping them to develop excellent technical skills that meet the needs of employers in the sector. Skills competitions can provide such opportunities to demonstrate exceptional skills.

This approach is not only applicable to education, but to business as well.

A growth mind-set developed across an organisation can lead to more innovation, higher quality products/services and a culture where they compete to convert and retain customers, increase revenue and gain more market share. It could also help increase brand awareness, increase the profile of the business and gain more positive publicity.

When looking at the focus of my growth mindset approach, I have develop the 7C model:

1. Curiosity

2. Courage

3. Commitment

4. Consistency

5. Compete

6. Collaborate

7. Celebrate

1. Curiosity

'I am neither especially clever nor especially gifted.
I am only very, very curious.'
Albert Einstein

Stay curious. It's an approach to life that provides interest, keeps life exciting, always with some intrigue.

Develop an inquiring mind, ask the questions, do your research, read, study, and explore.

Whatever interests you have in life or in your sector, don't ever settle and give up being curious - what's your goal, dream, vision of your one amazing life?

Don't be afraid to explore and enquire. What's out there? who does it well? What does excellence look like? Who do you admire? What have they achieved? Can you learn from them? Look at the ideas you have and where you can find knowledge and expertise, develop a genuine sense of wonder. A sense of wonder can be described as a combination of intrigue, curiosity, admiration, awe, questioning ...so many aspects. When you encourage a sense of curiosity, I feel it brings the magic to life. We want individuals to be intrigued about how to improve. How to make small gains. How to achieve excellence. Do they wonder how other individuals or organisations do it differently or better? What other opportunities are there? How do they keep evolving? How to keep improving and being better today than yesterday?

They may develop a feeling of joy in being adventurous, creative and innovative, as well as improving their performance, and ultimately being more successful. I also feel joy will be enhanced if you always look for humour in life, it's something I inherited from my father. He worked very hard, but always had a twinkling smile, with a dry Cumbrian sense of humour, which was appreciated by everyone he met. It's not healthy to be serious all the time, we need to be light-hearted when we can be, and where it's appropriate. To me, humour is absolutely essential to life, including in the workplace. There is definitely a time and a place, but many situations are enhanced by humour. It lightens the load and raises a smile, especially dry humour.

2. Courage

'All our dreams can come true,
if we have the courage to pursue them.'
Walt Disney

What comes first -confidence or courage? They are very intertwined. Do you embrace challenges and be courageous and in turn you develop much more confidence? Or do you need to be confident to even try and have a go, and in turn you get braver and braver and develop courage. Either way, embrace them both -be bold, have a go, try, lean-in and you will find both courage and confidence will increase.

I encourage everyone to embrace challenges – to see these as an opportunity for growth and learning. If your approach is one of continual learning, you can gain valuable lessons from simply having a go. Use the experience to give you feedback, reflect, and then try again. Using this approach helps you to improve, to grow and do better when you try again. Resilience, which can be termed mental toughness, can translate into competitiveness, so the more you compete and embrace whatever the results are, the more you learn and improve.

'Competition is the fuel that ignites innovation.'
Simon Sinek

The more you challenge yourself, and develop courage, the more resilient you will become. Many of us have an imposter syndrome – we think we're going to get found out, and people will know we're not sure what we're doing and are simply winging it. Have the courage to face your fears, what are you feeling insecure about?

If you reflect, you will realise you have the evidence to show how much you know, you have the expertise and skills, and all the positive feedback you have received. Appreciate the hard work you have put in, the hours of practice it has taken, how unique you are as an individual and why the world needs you to avoid shying away, and playing small, but to shine your light and light the way for others.

3. Commitment

'There are no secrets to success. It is the result of preparation, hard work, and learning from failure.'
Gen. Colin Powell

Commitment is usually explained as being dedicated to a cause or activity, or pledging to do something in the future. If we are to do something well it needs long term commitment. Firstly, you need to show up and engage with the opportunity. Many believe the world is changed by those who show up. Simply show up and be a person of your word.

If you're going to get involved in an opportunity, then go all in! Don't be half-hearted. Really put everything into it. If you're not fully committed and give it your all, how will you know what you're capable of? If you don't do well or achieve your goal, you'll blame yourself for not fully participating and feel you could have done better. Guilt will creep in, as you feel you let yourself down. Its better to go all out and give it your best shot, then if you don't get the outcome you wished for, you will know you did you very best, you will learn so much, which will fuel your next try. No guilt, just pride you gave it your all. Prepare to try your hardest. Fully participate. Don't hold back. It will take careful planning, detailed preparation, research into winners or those that have achieved the goal you are after, and lots of practice. It will serve you well if you can develop a strong desire to learn and develop new skills. You will be self-motivated and absolutely love the journey and the growth you achieve.

'Strive for excellence, not perfection,
because we don't live in a perfect world.'
Joyce Meyer

Hard work needs to be mentioned. There is no excuse for not working hard. You need to develop a great work ethic; this will serve you well in all aspects of life. A great deal of effort can be the path to success; focus on the process, the learning and development of skills, rather than the outcome.

A growth mindset believes that abilities and talents can be developed and strengthened through hard work, dedication and learning, rather than being fixed traits that you're born with. It's not about being flexible, open-minded and positive– that can be termed a false growth mindset. It also isn't about praising and rewarding unproductive effort, as this is never a good approach in any aspect of life.

4. Consistency

*'Our greatest weakness lies in giving up. The most certain way
to succeed is always to try just one more time.'*
Thomas Edison

Consistency is the key. Many believe success is all about consistency. With most things it is far better to do a little every day, than a lot once a month. There is huge merit in achieving small gains, these may only be 1% or less, but over time they make a huge difference. The term habit stacking is being used to describe how you schedule and link good habits one after another, with reminders as appropriate. This helps nudge you into doing the right things, without getting distracted. High performers in all walks of life are sharing how they follow their system, as opposed to a feeling or emotion. So, if one day you don't feel you have the motivation, or the discipline, just follow the process or system you have developed, without thinking about it. It's as if you're on remote control. Don't think, just do. Get your running shoes out the night before so it's easier to slip them on and go for a run in the morning. Leave a jug of water and glass near the sink so it's easy to increase your water intake. Arrange a lift to pick you up to go to the gym, then there's no excuses. Stack and align these good behaviours so you make it as easy as possible to do the things you are trying to make daily habits.

Consistency can develop resilience. Plan, prepare and then participate. You need to give it your all. It's not about competing with others; it might be that you're competing with yourself to be better today than yesterday. Don't stay in your comfort zone, as you can stagnate.

Take some risks, if it doesn't work out, fine, you will learn. Many successful people encourage you to fail fast: don't linger and procrastinate, try again, learn, move on, improve. Not trying is the only failure.

If you have more resilience, you can bounce back from failures, with renewed determination. It isn't worth worrying about perfection, it doesn't exist, we've all got flaws, we need to embrace them, after all its what makes us interesting and unique.

5. Compete

*'I release any feeling of competition or comparison.
I simply do my best and enjoy being me.'*
Louise Hay

Walt Disney said, *'I have been up against competition all my life; I wouldn't know how to get along without it'*. This reflects the concept that from the beginning of time many aspects of life are competitive. This could be way back when cave men were searching and competing for food and shelter, or more recently the competitive environment when applying for a job, or even the competition you are up against when promoting your own skill or business. Even though we may not want to be seen as very competitive, we must acknowledge that many facets of life have a competitive angle. If we embrace this, it can encourage people to do their best, learn, improve, and then do even better.

'Competition is always a good thing. It forces us to do our best.'
Nancy Pearcey

Balanced competitiveness can be healthy and lead to success in all aspects of life. It shouldn't be an aggressive competitive approach. You might be mainly competing with yourself, so you are better today than yesterday. Are you aiming to improve and grow, be it health, fitness, financial or other areas of your life? The main aspect is that you try, seek out competitive opportunities, so you have the chance to learn, improve and develop your resilience.

The New York Jets coach, Robert Saleh talked about the four levels of competitors that are found on every team:

1. **Survivors** - only do enough to get by (coasting, easy way out)

2. **Contenders** - motivated by external factors (money, fame)

3. **Competitors** - internally motivated to be the best regardless of the situation

4. **Commanders** - all that a competitor has, but brings people with them

This approach is fascinating whether you're in business or entering competitions, awards or for promotion. Its interesting to see that a true competitor is internally motivated, they will always try to do their absolute best and have a champion mindset. They are constantly looking to grow and learn, and react well to being coached. They aren't influenced by who they are competing against, that is a contender approach. It's also interesting to see that an educator could be a commander in that they have a champion mindset but take people (their students) with them on the journey. The least said about the survivors the better, but hopefully we could influence them to see the merits of moving towards a contender approach and beyond.

'Competition brings out the best version of oneself.'
Sheryl Sandberg

Another analogy about not focusing on the competition or battle, is the story of the crow who attacks an eagle by pecking at its neck. The eagle does not fight back but instead opens its wings and flies higher -eventually the crow can't breathe at the higher altitude and falls down. The key learning here is that not all competitions, battles or arguments need to be fought or responded to. Instead, have confidence, courage and commitment, take the higher ground, soar and leave everyone trailing in your wake.

6. Collaborate

'If you want to go fast go alone. If you want to go far, go together.'
African proverb.

Collaboration is closely tied to connection, and it is paramount. Many competitive opportunities can have an individual focus. However, there are plenty of situations where a team approach is essential.

This could be a team opportunity, with everyone working closely to achieve a goal. In this case everyone will have their role, playing to their strengths. Even if the activity is a solo opportunity there is often a team behind the player or competitor that contributes hugely to the success of the individual.

'Competition teaches you the value of hard work and dedication.'
Kobe Bryant

When planning your approach and seeking to deliver excellence there are many people who can support you. Where can expertise be found? Do your research. Seek help from others in your sector. Who are the experts? Who are known to be excellent in your field? Who has won awards, competitions, projects, business or promotions? Can you try new strategies or approaches? The phrase, *'It takes a village to raise a child'* highlights a team approach is essential in many situations. One person doesn't have all the answers. Therefore, you need to build a village around you that can support you to achieve your goal. Who might this be? Consider colleagues, educators, mentors, coaches, experts, specialists. Approach them, establish a rapport and see if they would be so kind as to help you on this journey. Always be grateful of any support and show consideration for their time, commitment and expertise. Share your successes as well as the disappointments; it's a team approach. Recognise and share the part they played in your success.

7.Celebrate

*'When we fail to acknowledge and celebrate small victories,
we get discouraged and the flame inside us starts to dwindle.'
Unknown*

Celebrate everything. Find joy in small wins.

Life can be challenging, and it can be bleak and joyless if we don't stop to look back and see what we have achieved. However small. Recognise your own progress, and that of others. If you're an educator or coach/mentor, recognise and praise hard work, commitment and progress. This provides encouragement. Sometimes the individual can't see how far they have come, and it can take them by surprise that someone can see their progress. It can spur people on to do more and be even better. It's not about 'winning', it's about celebrating that they took the challenge and entered, they tried, and there is learning and growth in participating. To be involved means you're building confidence, courage, resilience and skill.

If you win the award, competition, project, or business deal, there is still much to do, as its often a stepping stone to further opportunities, but take time to reflect, recognise how far you have come, and celebrate !

In a business situation, get to know your team really well, so you know what makes them tick and their motivation, values and goals. Be quick to praise, to recognise and celebrate hard work and good results.

If we're looking at how to develop a young person's resilience, research has shown that intentionally marking (celebrating) a positive life event will increase perceived social support. This is the belief that they have a social network that will be there for them in case of future, negative life events. This belief is associated with health and well-being outcomes, including increased life-span and decreased anxiety and depression. Life can be hard, let's look for the wins, however small and celebrate in whatever way you feel is appropriate.

You've probably heard the term social mobility, it's used to describe how individuals can improve their life outcomes, regardless of their background. It's my view that a combination of developing a growth mindset and embracing skills competitions, or other similar opportunities, is key to helping individuals improve their income, education and occupation. As I've mentioned earlier, the results can truly be transformational.

Life is short. Opportunities are everywhere. If you are lucky enough to get a chance to shine, in whatever way – take it ! Grab it with both hands. You've got nothing to lose – no downsides. It could be a competition, a project, an adventure, a business – just embrace it all. This is what life is all about, you don't just want to survive, you want to thrive and live the life you have dreamed of.

When you next get the opportunity – SHINE. The world needs more highly skilled, excellent individuals with resilience, who are continually learning and growing and making this planet a better place - that's you ! Don't waste a second.

'You were born to shine; don't ever let anyone steal your light.'
Matshona Dhliwayo

About Joan Scott

Joan is a Beauty and Spa expert, a skills consultant, and an award-winning educationalist. Her many roles in further education include Educator, Verifier, Examiner, Judge, Curriculum Manager, Director and Assistant Principal. She has a wealth of experience and knowledge of the post 16 education sector including full time programmes, apprenticeships, employability, adult and community learning. Joan has an MSc in Leadership.

As CEO and Chair of the Hair and Beauty Industry Authority (HABIA) Joan leads the team to develop national standards, apprenticeships, endorse high quality CPD courses and promote standards, education, excellence and professionalism.

Joan is author of The Official Guide to Spa Therapy and co-author of *Beauty and the Best* and *Fit for Purpose Leadership*. Recently she was lead author and editor of *Leading from the Heart*, where the authors share how they create profitable enterprises by putting their people and relationships at the heart of the business.

Joan is a Brand Ambassador for WorldSkills UK, a world-class skills network that embeds world-class training standards across the UK. She is passionate about the pursuit of technical excellence and the impact of skill competitions, in creating more opportunities for young people and delivering the high-quality skills that employers need'.

Joan supports organisations who want to focus on technical excellence and work closer with World Skills UK.

Joan.scott@skillsactive.com

Instagram: @joanscott__@habiauk

Linkedin: Joan Scott

The Struggle Within: Battling The Fear Inside

Kylie Denton

Have you ever truly asked yourself, "Am I happy?" Is this what life is all about? Is my purpose higher than this?

If I look back on my life 20 years from now, would I be happy with who I had become and what I had achieved?

Scary and deep, I know. Yet as much as I wished I could forget these questions, I just couldn't. They were conscious thoughts but there was something unconsciously happening to me as well. I am the type of person who can reflect deeply - even if it makes me uncomfortable - and boy, did these thoughts make me uncomfortable!

So, I leant into that discomfort and searched for meaning. I mean seriously Kylie, you are pregnant with your second child, and you are asking yourself these questions now? Why now - why not before you had children? Sometimes we don't get to decide when the thoughts arise, they just come (even when you don't want them to).

These questions continued to swirl in and out of my mind, toying with me as I went through my daily routines and creeping back in during moments of quiet.

They refused to be silenced, refused to be ignored. I had to ask myself – why?

On the surface, everything seemed perfect. I was married, we had a beautiful 3-year-old daughter named Sophia, and I was 16 weeks pregnant with our next daughter. But the truth was, I wasn't happily married, and I knew my husband wasn't truly happy either. I felt like I was destined for more, I was ambitious to the bone, he wasn't, we were so different in so many ways. Our values and beliefs were not aligned and the way we communicated was like we were in fact on different planets. You remember that book *Men Are From Mars, Women Are From Venus*? This book was absolutely written about us.

Now, I want to be clear that there is nothing wrong with going to work each day, coming home, doing mum things, and being a wife. Lots of people do it and they love it, and I love the fact that they do love it. I think there's often this sense of comfort and fulfilment in routine – in waking up, following a pattern, and enjoying the peace to be found in predictability. And that's more than OK.

But the beauty of being human is that we're all wired differently. And as much as there can be serenity in sameness for some – for others, what calls to us can be the opposite – this pull towards growth, change – and challenge that cannot be ignored. I know many people find fulfilment in routine, but for me, the act of routine was not a comfort. In fact, it felt like it was a cage. It felt like I was living the same day over and over, like in the movie *Groundhog Day*. I just wanted more.

I had this yearning that would not be silenced. I could feel it in my body – so much so that both my conscious and unconscious selves were speaking to me! I needed to lean into this. To sit in the grit as they say. To unpack it all.

It was clear that I wanted more from my life, that there was more to my story. And speaking of stories - I wanted to write, to share ideas with the world that inspired action. I had also dreamt of owning my own business, so I didn't have to put my children into daycare five days a week, all day. I wanted to have options, flexibility, holidays, to design a life that would support my search for more purpose, more gusto, more excitement. I wanted to become more than I was. Deep down, I knew that difficult decisions needed to be made to bring about the right conditions to support that beautiful 'becoming'.

When I became a parent, I realised the profound responsibility of being the guiding light in your children's lives. That critical role I get to play that illuminates the many paths they can explore, highlighting the endless opportunities the world offers. Through my guidance, they have the support to learn to navigate life's journeys, discover their own innate potential, embrace the adventures that await them.

I am in the humbling position of being able to nurture them so they can, one day, not only ask themselves the same questions that I was asking myself now - but to also have the courage to answer their own call - whatever that may be.

For me being married felt like the fire inside of me was dying. It wasn't a relationship that encouraged what I wanted or motivated me to improve myself and chase my dreams.

One Sunday afternoon, I was sitting in my back garden, and I remembered a quote I once heard, "when you are just EXISTING, life happens to you… and you manage, when you are truly LIVING, you happen to life… and you lead. The function of a human is to live, not to just exist.

I was purely existing… I knew I had to make a change. I remember thinking back to my father, Neil.

In 1976, he single-handedly brought up three girls — my sister Sherry was 10, Tracey was 7 and I was 3 years old. ALL by himself. I remember thinking if he can do it, I can do it too. It was such a powerful moment, I want to make it clear, I am not saying just because he was a man, and could do it then I could do it. It was more that moment of inspiration for me — that he raised my sisters and I all by himself (and we turned out alright I must say, ha ha). It was this thought that empowered me, that gave me this steely resolve — knowing that I had the strength inside of me to do it myself, too.

One day, looking in my bedroom mirror whilst sitting in my bed, I knew at that moment, I had to break free from the monotony and pursue my hope of what this life still had to offer me. I needed to not merely exist, but to live. I was no fool. I knew it wasn't going to be easy, but I was determined to create a life that I would be proud of. A life that, when I looked back on in 20 years' time, I would be proud of. A life that my children could be proud of, seeing their mother become who she was truly capable of being and helping them to see themselves in their future as just as capable.

The hardest part of ending a marriage is battling the internal horror stories you tell yourself.

You know, that inner narrator that we all have with a flair for the worst case scenario. The negative self-talk loops you can't free yourself from. The echo chamber of fear and self-judgement. These are just some of the shadow stories that my mind conjured up for me… trust me, I am just touching the tip of the iceberg here. They were raw, they were painful and they were terrifying. and the worst thing is, it's really hard to hold back your fears when you are already going through such a challenging time (And I am sure my pregnancy hormones were pushing the limits too!)

As brutal as these thoughts were, I knew that fear would only hold me back if I let it…

- Your children will be scared, and it will be your fault.

- You didn't stick it out for the kid's sake.

- You're making a mistake – you can't do this yourself.

- You should try harder; marriage isn't meant to be a bed of roses all the time.

- Your pregnancy hormones are causing this - it will pass.

- You are making this about you – you need to stay for the children.

- You can't do it by yourself; it will be too hard.

- You are making the biggest mistake of your life.

- You're going to fail and be left with nothing.

- Your children will grow up and blame you.

- You will psychologically damage your girls. (I have formal qualifications in psychology, so this particular fear felt very real!)

- You can't manage the responsibilities alone.

- You will be judged and talked about.

- Your friends will judge you, take sides and you will lose some of them. (Yes to both of the last two by the way. Not a loss at all really, now that I am past it.)

- Your children will grow up without a traditional family structure. (This was a concept I had always valued, despite not having experienced it myself. This was something I really had to deal with – I had to make a new family definition).

The fear and sleepless nights that these emotional ghost stories caused me were brutal. It was a really tough and draining time. There were many days as a single mum when I just longed to be my normal, happy, energised self, but it was hard doing it all alone.

My dad died when I was 13 years old and losing him was tough, don't get me wrong, but separating from my husband while 16 weeks pregnant was one of the most challenging periods of my life.

As the primary breadwinner, I faced the daunting reality that in order to keep our home I would be required to return to full-time work, necessitating placing both my daughters in daycare five days a week. I had always been in leadership roles, and leadership roles had always demanded more than the standard nine-to-five, promising long hours away from my children. This was so distressing for me; this was the opposite of what I was striving for in terms of trying to design a life with flexibility. The weight of these decisions was overwhelming, often bringing me to tears – tears of uncertainty, fear, and worry about the unknown.

Inviting back in all the unhelpful thought patterns I had, and that self-doubt soundtrack blaring at full volume that I was not able to do this myself, and I was setting myself up for failure.

Deep down, I'd always harboured the dream of working for myself. Yet, during my marriage, fear held me back – not just the fear of failure, but the immense pressure of being the main income earner. Ensuring my family could afford the things we valued and providing a stable home for our girls rested heavily on my shoulders.

One unexpected advantage of enduring a divorce while pregnant was the inability to resort to alcohol. There was no numbing the pain or escaping reality; I was left alone with my unfiltered thoughts, confronting them head-on. Some days, this raw introspection was shocking, but it was undeniably necessary. Even though the thoughts were tough to deal with, there was this deep feeling inside of me that knew that my chosen path was right - even though some days it sure didn't feel like it!

I remember sitting in my lounge room late one night, contemplating the possibility of starting my own business. With 20 years of experience in financial services, a strong network of colleagues, formal qualifications in psychology, credentials as a former financial adviser, and certification as a professional coach, the foundations were well and truly there.

The thought ignited a spark: What if I started my own business during maternity leave and observed how it unfolded? Although this was not the first time these thoughts had come to me, it was the first time I felt brave enough to think that this time it could be a real possibility.

The following day, I approached my boss to discuss the feasibility of pursuing personal ventures while on maternity leave. He informed me that as long as there was no conflict of interest, I was free to proceed. This revelation was both exhilarating and terrifying.

Over the next few weeks, I grappled with palpable fears – those that manifest physically, causing nausea, cold sweats, and a churning stomach. Sharing my aspirations with those around me got mixed reactions. Many questioned my timing, suggesting I return to a stable job to avoid excessive change during such a tumultuous period. While their concerns stemmed from care, I know some undoubtedly questioned my capabilities - or maybe it was their own fears surfacing and projecting onto me. This mirrored dynamics in my marriage, where I had yearned for encouragement to become my best self, yet never received it.

Ambition. Reflecting on this as I write this chapter, I recalled a CEO's insight from a recent CPA International Women's Day panel that I was fortunate to be a part of. She shared how supporting ambitious women is not only what uplifts us, but also what elevates those around us. It's infectious, supportive, and has the potential for this beautiful ripple effect if we embrace it.

There were many times when I was going through the process of being a new business owner where I questioned why it seemed to be so challenging for society to support those that are ambitious. Is it for many their own fears shining through? Is it their jealously?

Or is it them just not knowing how to lean into this themselves?

As a follower of Tony Robbins, I remembered his advice to ask oneself during challenging times, "What is great about this situation?" And I'm very much a glass half full advocate, too.

Had I not summoned the courage to leave my marriage and embrace instability, fear and the unknown, I might never have embarked on my entrepreneurial journey. This path led me to author and co-author seven books, build my own office, work with the most amazing companies and leaders all over the world, work and travel internationally with my children.

There is no denying it, the journey was fraught with stress, worry, and fear of failure, and there were many ups and downs as there is with most businesses, but it has taught me that I can do it, it has seen me dig deep into my resilience reservoirs and it has absolutely moulded me into the person I am today. I would not be half the person I am without going through all of this.

Today, my two beautiful daughters, Olivia, now 12, and Sophia, 15, are happy, brave and confident little ladies. They have this deep-seated belief that they too can achieve anything — a testament to the resilience and growth cultivated through adversity. I am so proud of who they are and of the women they are becoming.

They have witnessed firsthand the challenges and triumphs of embracing change and living authentically. They understand that life is not about avoiding difficulties, but rather about growing through them.

One recent Sunday afternoon, I was spending time with Olivia, my youngest. She sat on the lounge room floor watching YouTube Shorts while we folded laundry, and a conversation unfolded that I hadn't anticipated (but aren't they often some of the best kind?). The TV played a YouTube segment about life with divorced parents. Olivia glanced up and remarked, "I know what that's like." Curious and slightly apprehensive, I asked, "What's that like, honey?"

She turned to me with a bright smile and said, "It's GREAT." Taken aback, I chuckled lightly and inquired, "Why is it great?" Olivia's response warmed my heart: "Because I get to spend more time with you, and I love our family just the way it is, plus I don't have to share you with anyone."

In that moment, I realised that despite the challenges, our family had found a unique happiness, a rhythm – dancing to the beat of our own drum, if you will. I had created a family path, all by myself. Isn't it funny how we think that a family is automatically that nuclear sort of Utopia - the mum, dad and children. I did too, but in getting intentional about forging my own path, I had actually created a family path that my children loved too. They say happiness breeds happiness – and it warms my heart that I have cultivated an environment where opportunity, ambition and joy are infectious.

My ex-husband and I maintain a great relationship and for that I am forever grateful, especially for the sake of our children. He has the freedom to visit and call them whenever he wishes. Yet, they live with me full-time – a dynamic I cherish and am deeply grateful for.

This journey has taught me that life is indeed scary and unpredictable. Yet, when we believe in ourselves and actively shape our future, we tap into the power we all have within us to not only transform our own lives, but also to positively influence those around us, especially the young minds who look to us for guidance. It's legacy building – and it's a powerful and poignant responsibility.

Through my experiences that life has provided to me - running a successful business, collaborating with remarkable leaders worldwide, building a dedicated office, and delivering keynote speeches internationally with my children by my side - I strive to demonstrate to my daughters the power of a growth mindset. These endeavors highlight the opportunities that emerge from life's challenges and reinforce the importance of conscious leadership as both a professional mantra and an intentional, lived experience.

It is through this same level of consciousness and intention that I'm constantly excited by the future now – a future where I continue to get to work with like-minded professionals that care deeply about their craft, their clients, their teams, and the story they want to leave behind. Kindred spirits. Those who aren't complacent, who aren't afraid to lean into the future they want to create with lasting influence, cultures of trust, and leave a legacy of leadership and connection.

Reflecting on my own journey, I've come to realise that life is a series of choices that shape our paths. As I look ahead, I encourage you to reflect on your own journey. Are you living authentically? If you were to look back in 5, 10 or even 20 years, would you be proud of the person you've become and the risks you've taken? Are there choices you want to take, but are fearful?

Remember, it is not the challenges that define us – but rather how we rise above them.

I hope you choose to live life fully, embracing the moments where you are uncertain, scared or uncomfortable. I hope you pave the way for a legacy that you can be proud of.

About Kylie Denton

Kylie Denton is a leadership consultant, professionally certified coach, bestselling author, and keynote speaker, specialising in leadership and sales within financial services and government sectors, including education, healthcare, and childcare. With over 30 years' experience and formal qualifications in psychology, she partners with organisations across Australia to transform leadership and elevate client engagement.

Kylie's work sits at the intersection of leadership development and client connection — empowering financial services professionals, sales teams, and people leaders to boost performance, build trust, and drive results.

Known for her blend of deep coaching expertise and commercial acumen, Kylie challenges and champions her clients — helping good leaders and great client-facing professionals grow to the next level.

At her core, Kylie is a passionate advocate for the human side of business: fostering connection, trust, and values-led leadership.

kylie@performanceadvisorygroup.com.au

https://performanceadvisorygroup.com.au/

LinkedIn: https://www.linkedin.com/in/kyliedenton5/

https://www.linkedin.com/company/74288929/

Facebook page: https://www.facebook.com/softskillsau

Instagram: https://www.instagram.com/performanceadvisorygroup/

Level Up. Keep Up. Turn Up.

Candice Gardner

As someone fascinated by life's endless possibilities, and how humans can be capable of so much more than we think we are, I am keenly interested in the concept of self-actualisation.

It is widely acknowledged that accomplishment and achievement can bring joy, and purposeful activity is intrinsically linked to our contentment and sense of self. This is the manifestation of self-actualisation – the fulfilment of our potential, creativity and personal growth – and often defined or interpreted as success.

What constitutes success will be different for each of us. And thus, so will our views on when, how or why we might shine. Will we shine for just a moment? Or can we capture the essence of what it means to shine so that it travels with us always?

In my view, shining is about radiating self without compromise. Shining is about how we show up so that others can recognize our attributes, skills and impact. Shining is about standing out in all our unique glory. Yes, that is right… our glory! I don't mean over-inflated, inauthentic posturing. I mean proudly owning our brilliant skills, valuable knowledge, noteworthy attributes and meaningful contribution.

This is about everything that we are.

Take note though - who we are is not static. We are evolving all the time through our life stages and experiences. The places we go, the people we meet, the conversations and topics we explore all contribute to shaping and reshaping our opinions and behaviours. One moment in time will never really capture it all.

And so, this chapter is about much more than a moment. It is about feeling fulfilled as you travel through life, working towards shining as the best version of yourself at any moment in time. And most importantly, that you are embracing life and its many opportunities as part of the journey to realising all that you are.

In this chapter I will share a little of my own journey and experience and how that has led me to incredible adventures and several self-defining moments.

If we are shaped by our experiences and who we are is the sum of our experiences, then surely exploring new experiences is essential to expanding our unique view and contribution to the world. A route to helping us shine.

I see myself as a lifelong learner. A childhood filled with Readers Digest, National Geographic and books fuelled my curiosity in our world from science to nature to humanity. They helped develop my awareness that there is always more to learn, more to understand, and someone else's perspective to consider.

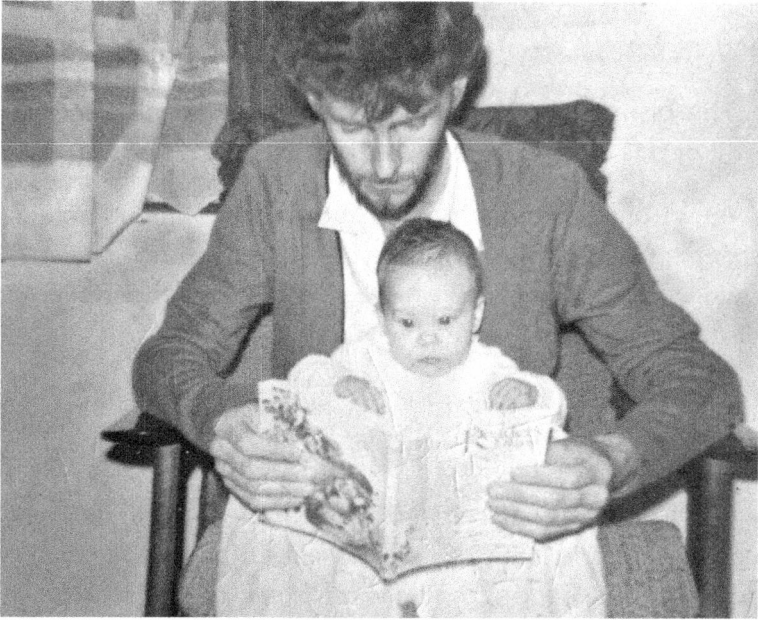

My Dad started reading to me early.

From school to college and into my first job - the learning did not stop. That first job as a skin and body therapist was a gift and set the tone for both my career aspirations and my professional expectations.

A work experience placement landed me a permanent position with Jenny Eales - gifted therapist and an industry OG. I got my first taste of continuous professional development under her and have a lot of wonderful memories being mentored by her and of traveling across South Africa to conferences and training.

Jenny's approach to business, her craft and her clients has stayed with me throughout my career. I will always be grateful to her for helping set foundations that have enabled my own career journey. I did not only learn about my industry and develop my skills, I discovered so much about who I am, what I value, and how to approach my life and career.

This brings me to explaining my personal mantra and the title of this chapter - *Level Up. Keep Up. Turn Up.*

As we unpack what this is all about, I recommend holding space for reflection. Consider your own approach and your own activities. Are you giving yourself every opportunity to discover, grow and shine?

Level Up

Level Up is about remaining open to learning. Learning could be completing further qualifications or attending courses, but it does not always need to be structured or formal training.

It could be listening to someone else's experience or reflecting carefully on your own. It could be receiving feedback or guidance from a mentor or someone more experienced. It could be reading and researching a topic yourself. The essential element is building on your knowledge and skills by adding new content and ideas to the scaffolding of what you already know.

The quote by Ray Kroc, the American businessman who franchised McDonalds', has stuck with me – *'When you're green, you're growing. When you're ripe, you rot'*.

Those who think they know it all are already on the decline. If you plan on shining, then declining is not an option. The very essence of self-actualisation is growth and personal development.

Learning has been a vital part of my work. Not simply because I have been an educator and trainer for over 25 years, but because I have been fortunate to learn from so many knowledgeable and skilled individuals along the way. I have developed my own skills as a practitioner, an educator, a manager and a leader. I am still learning daily, and I always consider how I will level up each year.

How will you level up? What knowledge and skills will take you to the top of your game? Do you prioritize your growth and learning?

Stay green, so you keep growing.

Keep Up

Keep up is all about recognizing that everything around us is constantly evolving. From science and technology to social changes related to health, wellbeing, quality of life and our environment. Innovation drives us forward, and mostly this results in progress.

If we do not make a concerted effort to stay engaged and keep up with how things are moving, we will be left behind as the world advances and moves forward. Regardless of what industry we work in, or in what situation we are trying to shine, relevance is everything.

Simply standing still is a disastrous strategy. We must move forward and keep pace, or we will find ourselves further and further behind. Keeping pace will enable us to make incremental shifts and agile pivots. These are generally easier than monumental transformations and definitely less daunting.

Change is necessary to adapt to the new context, so that what we are doing is still relevant.

Industry or trade media and events, conferences, and community conversations provide insights - listen intently, pay attention, engage... keep up.

We don't need to follow the crowd necessarily but to shine we need to understand the context in which we find ourselves.

So here is your next reflection...

Do you have ten years' experience... or one years' experience repeated ten times?

Whether we take two, five, ten or thirty years, if we do not remain open to learning, consistently building our knowledge, skills and experience, or if we fail to keep alert to changing times, we will likely find ourselves fairly close to where we started but unfortunately in an entirely different context.

Perhaps you have become disconnected or isolated in your work, and there is a need to shift gear. It might be useful to level up or to turn up, as both can help you reconnect.

Turn Up

Sometimes opportunities present themselves in really unexpected ways. Turning up is not about making appearances and simply turning up physically. It is about turning up mentally and emotionally, actively engaging, networking and being prepared to contribute.

This will enrich who we are and will enrich the lives and activities of others.

I know that when life gets overwhelming, we need to be able to say 'no'. Yet I always think carefully about what I say 'no' to. Does this present an opportunity or experience that I have not had before? Or one that I gained a great deal from previously? Whilst it might seem easier to just forgo the experience as it requires added effort, I may be able to rather make other trade-offs to allow me to participate.

Truthfully, I have never once regretted my decision to say 'yes'. I have learnt or discovered every single time. Often considerably more than the obvious. Here are some examples of opportunities and experiences I said yes to, and what I learnt or resolved to do.

'We need someone to be interviewed by BBC News' … okay, yes!

…reminded me how outdated many people's views of the professional skin care industry are!

I was driven to find opportunities for advocacy and ways to influence public opinion and policy; to join with other voices to champion the social and economic impact.

'Will you speak at the Learning Technologies Conference championing women in learning?' … would love to, yes!

…don't underestimate the value of wider networks and exploring great ideas from diverse sectors and communities.

I became proactive in seeking out different perspectives from other industries…

...oh, and I must exploit relevant tools as the digital learning landscape is exploding with innovation.

'Can you lead on our charity partnerships?' ... willingly, yes!

...reconnected with the importance of purpose and making time for what matters most.

I learnt that awareness is just the start. Practical steps and actions drive step change.

'Will you join the Princess Royal Training Awards Assessor Team?' ... absolutely, yes!

...discovered extraordinarily creative training strategies delivered one-to-one and at scale that delivered powerful outcomes.

I was inspired to find more innovative ways to build skills at all levels in both educational and commercial contexts.

'Will you write a chapter for this book?' ... of course, yes!

...challenged my communication skills and experienced firsthand the power of storytelling to connect and inspire.

I definitely learnt that we need more personal stories in every circumstance!

Naturally, I was honoured and proud to accept these invitations despite how daunting some were. I said "yes" because I knew the gain was going to be beyond my expectations. And certainly, many of these felt like moments I could shine.

As you endeavour to hone expertise, build a knowledge base and develop skillsets, you may well focus in the areas relevant to your work or ambitions. Focus is a powerful way to make structured steps forward.

However, I would caution that linear thinking can prevent real growth. Don't get trapped in a focus tunnel with no peripheral vision!

Look laterally to other sectors or parallel skills for inspiration. You might be surprised by what completely new experiences deliver. Keeping an open mind ensures we do not stifle creativity, limit perspectives or reduce possibility. This is also exactly what growth mindset is all about. And it is why turning up to new experiences and opportunities is the final part of my mantra.

There is compelling evidence on the neuroscience behind growth mindset. Research has uncovered the ability of the brain to build new neural connections. This neuroplasticity of the brain makes us capable of continued learning and relearning, enabling us to develop new skills and new thinking. We can change our views and opinions based on new or different experiences. And we can master skills with practice and training, even if we thought they might be impossible.

So, if you have been reluctant to accept invitations, or felt anxious about new experiences, think about how you might overcome the barriers to benefit from the gains. Perhaps partner with a colleague or friend so you don't turn up alone but make an effort to speak to new people. Or suggest a smaller way to participate initially so that time or experience don't limit you.

Try to say 'yes' to more opportunities and be sure to turn up!

I have one final recommendation. Get enough sleep! It is a priority for your health and your self-actualisation.

Those neuroscientists will tell you that committing all that learning and those experiences to long term memory requires enough sleep. Sleep is not just resting. It is essential in how we encode, consolidate, and recall memories. Sleep ensures every experience is adding to your unique sense of self.

Keep growing. Stay alert to change. Be an active participant and willingly engage. You never know who you might meet, what you might learn or what opportunity might present.

Embrace life and relish the journey to realising all that you are.

About Candice Gardner

With 30 years' experience in professional skin care and skin care education, Candice Gardner is an active advocate for technical and vocational training and participates widely in standards development and employer steering to advance the Beauty, Aesthetics and Wellness sector.

With a 25-year tenure at global skin care brand Dermalogica, Candice is an experienced leader in skin care service and skills-led education programme design and people development.

Candice is a Member of Council for the City and Guilds of London Institute and Princess Royal Training Award Alumna. Holding various advisory and committee roles, including for the British Association of Beauty Therapy and Cosmetology (BABTAC), she was recognised in 2023 with a BABTAC Beyond Award for contribution to industry.

LinkedIn linkedin.com/in/candice-c-gardner

Instagram @candicecgardner

SHINE

Life Landscape: Letting Go, Embracing The Unknown

Jacqui Lee

Age 7 years old, I already knew in my heart and mind I was to be a free spirit and follow adventure. One day, I proudly announced to my friends, I was going to travel the world, and live in France. So far, I have accomplished lapping the globe a couple of times, both professionally and personally, and living some time in other countries, I am yet to live in France! This may happen, my intuition remains fully alive at age 51 years.

Early on, I learned not everything is clear cut. Obstacles on our path, often we are required to take a creative adventure, a tapestry of different experiences, choices, steps forward, backwards and to the side. A dance steeped in determination, strength, heart, courage, spirit, adaptability, vision, positivity, the commitment to stay true to yourself, whilst designing your path. In contrast to what we are taught, there isn't a set timeline to achieve certain life milestones, not all our markers need to be the same, and each one of us will be taking a different route to hit personal achievement. This is something I came to learn later in life, in my forties when time was not on my side to have a family of my own. The paths, choices, timing, stars aligning, I began to question my decisions, the challenges I had overcome, the speed I lived my life, my perfectionism, ME.

Leaving school, I went to college and trained as a Beauty Therapist and Hairdresser, having a very successful 33 years career, and counting, in the Beauty, Spa & Wellness industry. I have covered the length and breadth of the sector, starting at grass roots, into education as a Lecturer, Internal Verifier and Training Management for some of the most prestigious spas and skin care brands. All amazing opportunities, with the help of who I call my industry fairy godmothers, along the way they opened pathways to promotion, opportunity, providing confidence, ultimately leading me to accomplish a privileged position in the Consultancy Division within ESPA. ESPA were by far the most expansive developmental years of my career, travelling globally project managing new spa builds and openings for brands such as Ritz Carlton, Peninsula and Four Seasons hotels. Since 2013 I have worked for myself, and will be recognised in the industry as helping to revive the UK Spa Association, and collaborating with conferencing businesses to help get their event off the ground, grow and become successful.

You are so lucky! This is a phrase I have heard on many occasions. Yes, I have accomplished a wonderful career, my mum instilled I was to always have my own money, choose a flexible career so that I can work in and around changes within my life. During my early teens I came to learn, 7 years old me couldn't quite be as free as my imagination lead me to believe, I needed to create freedom from the limitations of my circumstances, and our family circumstances came with ill health from both my parents, long term, over a

15 years period for my dad, and intermittent with my mum. Leaving college, my first job was a 'clipped' version of what I really wanted to do, each job after that, was the same. They were all amazing opportunities, I maximised every part of each role and brand, not leaving a stone unturned, this is how I continued, over achieving, delivering and working. I was always making the most of everything, in my mind, I was unable to be completely free in the world and see what the universe may hand to me. It was through striving and determination, whilst emotionally handling my personal circumstances, that I built my inner strength and resilience, gaining my title the 'ballsy' one, or the one with 'grit'.

These days, I am still happy answering to either!

Being so committed to my career, it simply became a huge part of my identity. The industry was my security, my safe place, a space where I excelled, used my energy and outlet for over delivery and perfectionism. I was so immersed, too terrified to step away to have a family, which I assumed would be a part of my life journey. Personally, I felt a void in my life by not having children, and thought I made a huge mistake, where had my head been? Was I right to be terrified of giving up, and potentially losing everything I had ever worked for? What was to follow was a huge grieving process, starting in my early 40's, this got me caught in a loop for a few years, then the pandemic hit.

The pandemic saved me, a devastating and traumatic time for so many, my experience of this historic event, finally made me STOP. I got to sit still, evaluate, regroup, spend time in nature, unknowingly finding myself in meditation.

I invested in online personal development courses, at one point I had seven on the go, I had not yet learned to stop overworking and overdelivering! I even retrained to be a Quantum Energy Law of Attraction Coach, an intense long course with many hours of coaching clients, and modules to complete. This precious time to work on myself, peel back the layers, truly uncover my coping strategies, it began to set me free from thinking I had made mistakes in my life choices, learn they were not terrible errors to be filled with regret, they were decisions made with the options and limitations within life at the time. These learnings, also turned out to be the biggest bedrock of knowledge, renewed wisdom and strength, I was yet to realise I needed.

Hello menopause! Having emotionally accepted not having children, I am about to learn I will no longer be the woman I had always known. It came as a huge shock, it is an area in life we are not fully educated. I used to joke to my friends, I will be the one woman who will defy science, and still be fertile in my 90's.

There really was a part of me that believed it to be a possibility, how amazing if the woman was me! Alas, my experience was far from graceful, I didn't have much of a gradual decline, I was catapulted off a cliff. A freefall into a body and mind I knew nothing about, who on earth am I now? Physically, I experienced terrible symptoms, sickness, migraines, sleepless nights from hot flushes, eating up to four times during the night, I took midnight feasting to a whole new level (so hungry), brain fog, serious fatigue I did not recognise myself at all. Long gone was my sharp active, million mile an hour brain, my adventurous and slightly sporty body, unable to barely put one foot in front of the other, this is no way any woman should be living her life, a woman on her own, with financial responsibilities to uphold, how have the government not invested in science and research supporting women through?

Tapping into my resilience, frantically trying to cling onto my identity, I pretty much crawled into my local gym, desperate to get my life, as I knew it back on track. I did an enormous emotional meno dump on a young female instructor, who was at least 25 years away from experiencing my new reality, she patiently listened and made me feel I could pick my way through. True grit got me showing up at the gym, most mornings with zero sleep, often I was a ball of steam moving around (serious hot flush issue), I was determined to flush these hormones out of my body, and return to me again. Quickly, I learned my optimism alone will not work this time, I am still unable to defy science, this isn't quite the right path, re-navigate and take HRT, bingo! I continued with the gym, nearly 4 years later I have come a long way with my fitness.

Within two months of reclaiming parts of myself, next the ultimate test of strength was about to hit, and hit hard. Remember me saying my career became a huge part of my identity, the industry was my security, my safe place, a space where I excelled, used my energy and outlet for over delivery and perfectionism? One day, I was within a professional industry environment, when the rug was completely pulled from under my feet. An incident happened, one in which no male or female should ever experience. I am unable to voice details, I can only explain how utterly shattering the impact this has had on my life.

I thought I'd armed myself with strength, new learnings, new ways of coping, I was about to hit top level learning, get through each day, how to piece myself together, multiple times. This period of time, has by far been the most challenging of my life, my safe space not so safe anymore, a loss on many levels, loss of direction, personal financial loss, another loss of my identity, where do I fit now? How can I control keeping hold of everything I have ever worked for? The pain, has been very real.

Staying defiantly optimistic, I had to focus on what I could control in my life, that was sport, the gym and throwing all my energies, positive and not so positive, into training. What was to unfold, is miraculous. As a turning 50 birthday challenge for myself, I entered a global endurance race, consisting of running and functional exercises with heavy weights, for example a 50 metres sled push, loaded with 152kg. I thought of this race as a fun challenge, until I found myself on the podium and qualifying for the World Championships! It was such a surprise, 4 weeks later I flew to Nice in France (I have looped back to France again) to race against the fasted 50-54 years old PRO women in the world. Out of 225,000 competitors, only the fasted 2% got selected. At the championship, I assumed I would be at the bottom of the leader board, I was shocked to land in the top 1/3, could this be a new path opening? A new calling?

I'm a planner, I haven't planned this, but I think I should try again in the next season. Following the unknown path, podiums and winner flags continued, I qualified for the June World Championships, this year in Chicago, USA. During 2024/25 series there were 500,000 competitors, for this championship, only the top 1% got selected, with my recent PB race time, I am within the top ten fasted 50-54 years old women in the world, how crazy is that?

By distracting myself from what felt like two losses, an entire new world opened up for me, sport became my saviour, focus, outlet and purpose. It has been a path which appears to keep unfolding naturally, I have surrendered to allow it to happen. It has come with new experiences, discoveries of myself, people, adventures and what feels like sprinkles of magic popping up all the time, I am embracing it all the way.

I recently heard the quote 'sport doesn't build character, it reveals it'. Far from losing my career and identity, my success within endurance racing has strengthened everything. Winning over the last year, I finally discovered the feeling of living 'unclipped', there is nothing stopping me, the skies the limit, the world my oyster, I felt lost at first, unsure what to do with the freedom, I have never lived so free.

My true age 7 essence has been un-leashed!

Life really is an adventure, you grow through what you go through, everything is a learning, let go of control, allow room for magical mysteries, look for the glimmers, follow your heart, there is always hope, let the path unfold, and above all, SHINE.

About Jacqui Lee

Jacqui has over 30 years of experience in the Beauty, Spa, Wellness and Sport Therapy sectors. Utilising every opportunity to learn, she quickly climbed through the industry hierarchy, leaving in her wake, notoriously high standards.

Her wealth of industry knowledge and worldwide travel, has been advantageous the last 12 years. Reviving the UK Spa Association, then supporting Global and UK conferencing brands, connecting industry professionals at CEO, Director and Manager level, to strengthen knowledge and celebrate success.

Through Global endurance racing, Jacqui has expanded her connections in sport and fitness, uniting the wellness and fitness sectors in an exciting, visionary way.

Alongside athlete training for global racing and CrossFit, you will find her up a mountain, by the sea, writing, or enjoying a nice meal with friends, and of course a glass of bubbles, or a cocktail here and there!

jacquilee@me.com

LinkedIn: www.linkedin.com/in/jacqui-lee-321a1712

Instagram: @jlwellness

Naivety Is My Superpower

Fiona Jackson

Naivety often gets a bad rep. When we hear the word, we often associate it with inexperience, vulnerability, a touch of foolishness or even a lack of worldly understanding. Personally, I see it as my superpower. That instinct to jump in (sometimes, quite literally in my case), to say yes without overthinking, to trust that I'll work it out has shaped who I am and everything I've achieved.

Agreeing to try my hand at writing and create this chapter is a perfect example of that 'just say YES' mentality... so you might need to bear with me as I find my writing style.

Looking back, my fearless streak – the one that says 'just say yes' before any kind of logic kicks in first showed up in 2001. I stepped onto a train, leaving my boyfriend (now husband of 16 years, so long distance relationships can work) and my parents, with no idea when I'd see them again or what lay ahead for me as I embarked on my journey into the luxury Spa world with Steiner. I can't lie; I did have doubts, I was scared, I cried at times, but I had a DREAM and nothing was going to stop me from achieving it!

This was me truly stepping outside my comfort zone and I've done it many times since because, guess what, amazing things happen when you say YES to opportunities and dare to believe in yourself.

During my time onboard MS Norwegian Sun, I learned resilience, adaptability and what it truly means to deliver a world class customer experience. My boss, Todd, told me that when he first met me, I was a young girl, but he was watching me leave as a young woman. Back then I didn't fully understand what he meant, but when I look back, I absolutely do. The 11 months I worked for Steiner shaped me as an individual, as an adult and as a therapist. Although I didn't know it at the time my experiences were moulding me and laying the foundations for the business owner I was to become.

The second time I stepped outside my comfort zone was when I took the leap and opened my salon, Diva, in 2003. Driven by sheer determination and a 'what can possibly go wrong?' attitude, this is where I started to see my superpower really kick in! I was naive, I had no real fear and above all else I was determined to make it work. I had to learn so many new skills: advertising, financials, leadership - the list was long, but this is where I discovered the power of a growth mindset. Each challenge that I faced was an opportunity to learn and improve on what I was doing.

One day at a time I grew as an entrepreneur and developed my business. One of my biggest achievements in these early years was applying for a Prince's Trust loan to support my first premise move. I applied for the highest amount available, something my advisor from the trust tried to steer me away from as he'd never seen it awarded before. But I knew what I needed and wasn't prepared to settle for the easier option. I pitched my business plan to a panel of local business owners (Dragon's Den style!)

and was awarded the full amount. It was a bold move so early on in my business journey, but it paid off.

I progressed further, built a team, moved premises again, won awards and 21 years later I still have some of my very first customers as clients, but also as friends. We have been through so much in our 21 years together! This industry has given me a truly wonderful opportunity to learn about people, their needs, their wants and their desires. I have been lucky enough to have watched and supported clients through some of life's greatest highs and lows. I have also, at points, had the privilege of watching and supporting clients SHINE in their own careers and life goals. To be able to help lift others, create a safe space for them and support them when they need it most is a part of the job that I didn't know existed when I started out, but I now view it as one of my biggest privileges in life.

Whilst I was continuing to develop as a business owner, I decided that I needed a new challenge in life. Well, if I'm really honest, it wasn't a decision as such! After a few glasses of wine on a family weekend away, I agreed to swim two miles in Lake Windermere for charity. Only problem? I wasn't a swimmer. I didn't even own a swimming costume! But, true to form, I threw myself in – bought a costume, booked myself some lessons, and my swimming journey began.

I slowly built my distance in the pool then wriggled and fought myself into a wetsuit for the first time (if you've ever tried, you'll know!). I'd also like to point out that I live in Scotland so our water rarely gets to what I could describe as a comfortable temperature, so it was a real shock to the system when I first got in.

However, with the support of family - and yes, these were the same people who had questioned my abilities and thought I was mad to attempt the swim in the first place - I swam, floated, coughed and spluttered my way to the finish line... and within a week I was signed up for my next event! I had been bitten by the bug and wanted more. I adore the water, I love the calmness it gives me, the quiet in my busy mind but also the challenges it presents me with.

I completed quite a few swims in the years that followed, each one a challenge, whether it was the location, the distance or the timeframe. In 2018, I went even further – joining an all-female relay team to swim the English Channel. The voices around me were loud: *'You can't do that', 'You're mad', 'What are you thinking?',* but they only fuelled my fire. I have learned over the years never to allow other people's doubt time in my head. To believe in yourself is not always easy, especially when the voices around you are often louder than the one within. Self-belief is a powerful tool so it's important to keep believing, keep showing up, keep your vision and good things will happen.

After a year of brutal training - early morning sea swims in North Berwick (sometimes in hailstones), endless pool sessions, medicals, qualifying swims, training in the dark... we did it!

On October 3rd, 2019, we reached France after 16 hours and 14 minutes in the water. It's still my biggest physical achievement to date. Made possible by the people who said I couldn't, my sheer determination and yes, a healthy dose of naivety, because if I had known the reality of what it was going to be like I don't think I'd have got in the water to begin with!

Fast forward to 2023, and I relied on my superpower once again - can you see the pattern? A friend and I decided to push ourselves with a new challenge: a 25K swim for him and 20K for me in Loch Lubnaig, my Saturday morning happy place. Our friend Scott became our coach - Coach McQuade and quickly found his groove with his phrase *'right arm, left arm, repeat'* becoming my new mantra! It's worth noting that at this point my longest swim was 7K, but I jumped in and said yes to the challenge, not knowing if I was physically or mentally capable. Something that helped was the recollection of one of my husband's colleagues describing me as a 'force of nature' during my Channel swim training. It's one of the best compliments I've ever received, and strangely from someone I've never even met!

A full year of training followed – tracking nutrition, working with physios and personal trainers. The journey attempting to become a successful marathon swimmer was not an easy one. However, on 26th August, and after committing to increase my distance to 25K, at 6.33am, we set off in Loch Lubnaig to see if it was possible.

Nearly 13 hours later, I walked out of the water – I say walked, because getting yourself upright after being horizontal for nearly 13 hours of swimming is no mean feat. It was the greatest mental challenge I've ever faced and entirely self-inflicted – being alone in your own head for such a long time, questioning everything….and why? Because I wanted to see if I could; it's that simple! I never feel the need to compete with anyone else, the challenges I set myself, I have discovered are more than enough to fuel me in life, but I do enjoy rising to a challenge now and then.

Indeed professionally, one of my proudest moments was

taking my team to London for the Professional Beauty Awards in 2023 and 2024. Standing amongst the best in the industry as finalists was such an honour and, if I'm honest, a real pinch me moment! We didn't take home the win, but I believe what we gained from the whole experience was far more valuable. The fun of choosing outfits, the journey to London, the buzz of the champagne reception – we were celebrating everything we've built together as a team. We came back to Scotland without a trophy, but with fantastic memories, pride and a stronger belief in ourselves as a team, and as a business owner, I really couldn't ask for anymore.

In 2024, I asked a question. A question, that if I'm honest, I thought was a long shot but guess what? The belief in myself, my abilities and my determination to make change happen saw Professional Beauty Glasgow agree to have me as a speaker! It was an amazing experience; it opened a whole new world for me, new people, new confidence and a fresh direction. Asking that question has a lot to do with where I am now in my career path.

Cut to the present day and I'm writing this having pitched my RISE programme at the Professional Beauty London Future Focus Awards in March 2025 - I didn't win. There was only meant to be one winner, but the judges saw something in me. My passion. My determination. My RISE programme - designed to support the next generation of therapists. And they created a second place – just for me! This again brings me back to my superpower – I chose to stand on stage at PB's largest event and pitch in front of some of the industry's biggest hitters. That's the power of naivety. If I'd thought too much about what it meant to stand on that stage, I might never have done it.

But I did, and I now get to create my RISE programme, an accredited course due to launch in October this year!

This experience was a great life lesson and a strong reminder that winning should never just be about achieving first place! True success comes from the opportunities that we create from these experiences. It's in these moments, where we show up for ourselves, that we learn, grow, strengthen our resolve and ultimately become winners!

I have overcome obstacles, I have faced setbacks, I have failed, and I have developed resilience which I know isn't uncommon. However, what I have learned is that my naivety, my 'just say yes' attitude is my greatest asset.

Not a sign of ignorance, but a fearless belief that anything is possible and with that mindset I believe this is what allows us to SHINE!

About Fiona Jackson

Fiona Jackson is a passionate mentor, speaker, and beauty industry expert with over 21 years of experience as a successful salon owner. Committed to raising industry standards, Fiona supports salon owners in creating exceptional customer experiences and building businesses they're truly proud of. She is the founder of the RISE programme, an innovative training and mentoring initiative designed to bridge the gap between education and industry for newly qualified beauty professionals. Known for her practical, down-to-earth approach, Fiona inspires others to cut through the overwhelm and unlock their full potential. She regularly shares her insights through speaking opportunities, magazine features, and industry events, and was proud to be invited to Scottish Parliament for the launch of BABTAC's T.I.M.E initiative. Whether she's mentoring one-to-one or speaking to a room full of business owners or students, Fiona's goal is always the same - to raise standards and transform the way the beauty industry nurtures both its professionals and its clients.

www.instagram.com/fionajacksonmentor

www.linkedin.com/in/fiona-jackson-diva

hello@fionajackson.net

www.fionajackson.net

Shine Without The Suit

Arif Isikgun

There wasn't a big launch. No ribbon-cutting, no LinkedIn announcement, no cheering from the sidelines. Ai Beauty Consultancy was born in silence – just me, a laptop, and a quiet but persistent knowing: *if I don't do this now, I might never.*

From the outside, people often see the highlight reel. They see the polished version. The part where things look like they've clicked. But what they don't see – what they often don't want to see – are the long shadows that came before the shine.

They don't see the closed doors. The polite rejections. The emails left unanswered. The countless times I showed up for others only to find no one showing up for me. They don't see the confusion of wondering why the industry I had poured so much into – years of work, loyalty, passion – seemed to quietly turn its back when I decided to step out of the traditional mould.

There were many moments where I questioned everything. I hadn't just left a job. I had left a system. One where I'd been trained to be a certain way, speak a certain way, dress a certain way. I had been 'the right fit' until suddenly,

I wasn't. When I stopped performing and started showing up differently - more human, more emotionally open, more me- there was silence. A wall. No invitations. No support. No real conversation. Just a lot of suits and surface - level smiles. No one reached back when I reached out.

It hurt. Deeply. There's something uniquely painful about realising the room you once contributed to no longer sees you. Or worse - chooses not to. But that pain also gave me something I never expected: a lesson I couldn't have learned any other way.

The Real Meaning Of Resilience

Resilience gets thrown around a lot, especially in leadership and business circles. But in my experience, it's not about pushing through and pretending you're fine. It's not about staying the same and fighting harder.

Real resilience is evolution. It's the quiet decision to keep going, not in spite of what's happened, but because of what you've learned. It's staying open to growth, even when you're bruised. Especially when you're bruised.

I had to grieve what I thought my career would be. I had to sit with the disappointment. I had to stop looking for rescue and start looking inward. And slowly, quietly, I started rebuilding. Not to prove anything to anyone else - but to prove to myself that I could do it my way.

The Quiet Build

Ai Beauty didn't arrive fully formed. It came in phases - many of them messy.

In the early days, I didn't have a grand plan. I had skills, experience, and a gut feeling that the way we train, support, and empower people in beauty and wellness could be better. So I said yes to everything. Strategy decks. Spa audits. Retail training. PowerPoint presentations for brands trying to tell a story they hadn't fully figured out yet.

And while doing all of that, I was listening.

I paid attention to what made people light up. I noticed when something I said helped someone shift their mindset, reframe a fear, or try something new. I saw how many people in the beauty industry were craving something deeper. Not more rules - more connection.

Then came the messages. Quiet DMs from therapists who felt stuck in their roles. Questions from founders who wanted their teams to understand the 'why', not just the product features. Managers who knew their staff had potential but didn't know how to unlock it.

That's when it clicked. Ai Beauty wasn't just a consultancy - it was a space. A safe, human, intelligent space for people to grow. To feel seen. To unlearn the old rules and create new ones that honoured who they were.

When Nobody Shows Up

There's a particular loneliness that comes with stepping out of line - especially when you've spent years being praised for staying in it.

When you stop nodding along, when you start questioning what's always been done, when you offer something new - you become a bit of a threat. Not because you're aggressive or disruptive, but because you're holding up a mirror. And not everyone wants to see their reflection.

I thought the people I'd supported over the years would reach out. That old colleagues and clients would be curious or even cheering me on. But the silence was deafening.

In the past, I might've taken that as a cue to shrink. To change again. To make myself more palatable. But this time was different. This time, I decided to keep going without applause. To rebuild my confidence through action, not affirmation.

I stopped trying to earn a seat at tables I no longer believed in. I started building my own.

And crucially, I began asking for help - with no pride, no performance. Just honesty.

I connected with mentors outside of beauty. I joined communities of entrepreneurs, coaches, creatives - people who were also building something honest from scratch. And slowly, those relationships became lifelines. Not because they gave me a roadmap, but because they reminded me I wasn't alone in wanting to work differently.

Letting Go Of The Suit

The biggest shift wasn't external – it was internal.

I used to believe that in order to be respected in business, I needed to be 'corporate'. Suited, sharp, and always one step ahead. That belief ran deep. I had spent years trying to look the part, sound the part, be the part.

But somewhere along the way, I realised that wasn't my power. My power wasn't in how well I could conform. It was in how honestly I could connect.

So I let go of the suit - not just literally, but mentally. I stopped performing professionalism and started practising presence.

I began showing up to meetings with more curiosity than certainty. I started training with more empathy than authority. I created materials that made people feel - really feel- something.

And you know what happened? People responded.

Therapists who were scared to recommend products started asking better questions and building trust. Retail staff stopped "selling" and started storytelling. Brand founders found clarity - not through spreadsheets, but through reconnecting with their own purpose.

It turns out, what people needed wasn't more polish. It was more permission to be real.

Empowering Others To Shine

That's what my work is now. Creating permission. Creating space and creating connection.

Whether I'm working with a spa team, a solo founder, or a global brand, my goal is the same: to help people remember who they are - and give them tools to express that with clarity and courage.

Through this, I have been empowered to rise to unexpected heights – speaking on global stages, being viewed as a thought leader, and pathing the way for industry change as a touted experience in my field.

My trainings don't come with scripts. They come with stories. My workshops don't just hit KPIs. They build confidence.

And my Retail Excellence course, of which I'm beyond proud, which started as an experiment, has now helped hundreds of people double – or even triple – their sales. Not because they became better sellers, but because they became better connectors. They learned how to hold a conversation, not a script. How to tell a story, not push a product, and more than anything, how to emotionally connect.

Helping others shine isn't about giving them a formula It's about helping them find their way.

Redefining Success

When I started Ai Beauty, I thought success meant visibility. Recognition. Being accepted into the rooms I used to be shut out of.

Now I know better.

Success, to me, is when a therapist messages me to say they recommended a product with confidence for the first time.

It's when a founder tells me that I have enabled them to finally find the words to explain what they do and why it matters.

It's when someone sits across from me, eyes wide, and says, "I've never said this out loud before, but I think I'm ready."

That's success. That's the shine I care about now.

What I Know For Sure

If there's one thing I've learned, it's this:

- You don't need a title to be powerful. You just need to use your voice.

- No one will give you permission to be yourself - you have to claim it.

- Growth isn't about perfection - it's about momentum.

- Rejection often leads you back to yourself.

- And sometimes, the version of you they ignore is the version the world needs most.

Shine Anyway

The biggest myth in business is that we have to be polished to be respected.

But the truth is: *people connect to real, not perfect.*

The most magnetic individuals I've worked with weren't the loudest. They weren't the most polished. They were the ones who were deeply in tune with their purpose. The ones who led with story, not ego. Who shared vulnerably. Who weren't afraid to say, "I don't know, but I'll learn."

That's what I try to be every day. Not a flawless leader. A real one.

We don't need more perfection in this industry. We need more truth.

More courage.

More permission.

Permission to rewrite the script.

To challenge what's always been done — even if it ruffles feathers.

To stop performing, and start connecting.

To lead with presence, not polish.

To let heart be the strategy.

We rise when we give others the space to be seen. And we rise higher when we allow that same space for ourselves.

So if you're waiting for a sign, for approval, for someone to say it's okay.

This is it.

Shine anyway.

Not in spite of who you are - but because of it.

About Arif Isikgun

Arif Isikgun is an award-winning thought leader in the luxury spa and beauty space. As founder of Ai Beauty Consultancy and creator of Retail Excellence – a Habia-endorsed training programme – he has helped hundreds of therapists double or triple their sales through emotional connection, not pressure.

With 17 years in world-class environments like Harrods, Selfridges, and Aman spas, Arif blends commercial insight with emotional intelligence to transform how beauty professionals educate, connect, and sell. His work empowers teams to move from transactional selling to transformational client care.

Partnering with global brands and boutique founders, he designs learning strategies that build confidence, shift mindsets, and inspire performance through presence, permission, and purpose. Arif is especially passionate about helping therapists overcome the fear of retail, turning recommendation into a confident, human experience.

Trusted across the UK, Europe, and the US, Arif leads training, consultancy, and activations that drive growth and brand loyalty from the inside out.

Linked: www.linkedin.com/in/arifisikgun

Instagram: https://www.instagram.com aibeautyconsultancy

SHINE

Light And Legacy

Andrea Simpson

*'Experience and knowledge hold little or no value if kept to yourself.
Their true worth is only revealed when shared.'.*
Andrea Simpson – Facialist

Honesty...

In writing this chapter I reflected deeply. I find it much easier to see the light in others and the energy they create around themselves, than recognising it in myself.

I had to look at who has influenced me over the years, who I looked up to personally, professionally, the reasons why I admired them and the light they brought to me.

All those people 'shine with others', not above them. They have a way of lighting up a room with such energy and aura that just makes everyone around them see something great about themselves. I did ask myself, what does it mean to truly shine? Is it helping others rise along the way?

The easy option writing this, would have been to wax lyrically, sprinkled with anecdotal stories of my adventures, creating an illusion of perfection and Instagram check-ins, with visions of many of the incredible experiences in my work and personal life, that have significantly pieced together the jigsaw of my career.

The Long Road...

Getting to where I am now as a recognised and respected Facialist, businesswomen, key opinion leader (KOL), author and mentor didn't happen overnight. Even writing that description makes me think 'is that really me?' It's been a very long road that needed resilience to overcome setbacks with driven perseverance and ambition to overcome 'the imposter syndrome' that can creep up on us all, if we let it.

For many years I was an International Training Manager. A truly incredible experience that not only took me around the globe training the best spa teams in the world, but it was also a very special role that I had dreamed of doing for so many years and one I was very honoured to do.

Staying as a guest at these luxurious hotels, enabled me to experience first-hand the luxury touches they delivered so well. Making every moment so very memorable. However, as an educator I had the privilege of seeing the hard work 'back stage' that was needed to ensure the guest experience was exemplary, not just in spa, but the whole engine of the establishment from housekeeping to security and everything in between.

I remember fondly doing the pre-opening training for the Mandarin Oriental in Milan, where I spent three beautiful weeks. Towards the end I was invited to dine with the General Manager and department directors at their Michelin Star Chef restaurant. Before sampling the gourmet taster menu as the chefs, sommelier, maître'd and service team simulated opening evening, I sat in the bar of this incredible hotel, watching the talented bar staff perfecting cocktail after cocktail with exquisite alchemy.

So many stories and memories fill my head and heart like that, but there was a trade-off. I lived out of a suitcase; I was never at home. I spent more time in hotel beds (albeit very luxurious) than I did my own. I missed birthdays, anniversaries, weddings, but the one thing that really broke, me was being stuck overnight in New York after a flight cancellation. My son was leaving home the next day, relocating many miles away for a new job, new apartment and independent life. I didn't make it home in time. That was very hard and I feel emotional again thinking about it. It was a very long flight home the next day, knowing I was going home to an empty nest.

Whilst training the spa team at the Ritz Carlton Bahrain, I had been there nearly three weeks and was on the last few days of training when I became quite seriously ill. Within a few hours, I was in hospital being prepared for emergency abdominal surgery, alone, as a woman in a middle eastern country. I wasn't intimidated by this, having been a very independent and self-sufficient traveller from the age of 18, but it did feel quite frightening undergoing surgery alone in a foreign land.

I was very well looked after by the hospital. The Ritz Carlton was amazing in how they cared for me after leaving the hospital. The long journey home still holds some trauma for me today. I don't know how I managed that journey a few days post-surgery. Thankfully due to the amount of travel I did, I was able to upgrade my flights to business class.

I had to tell you about those experiences, because they convey the highs and lows of a job that I really loved. Every single moment was a life memory and I was so honoured to have done. I hasten to add I was fully informed and aware of the commitment and sacrifices to do the role and grasped the opportunity with both hands.

It tested my resilience, brought improvisation and challenges of teaching that excited me and I wouldn't be where I am today without them. I do have to add at this point, having my family's support and belief in me kept me going. They missed me yet were selfless with their generous encouragement for me to fly, grabbing every opportunity and experience I could. Thank you, you precious people for that, you know who you are.

The Spark That Fuels Me...

When I won the British Association of Beauty Therapy and Cosmetology (BABTAC) Facialist of the Year it was (and still is) the pinnacle of my beauty career and one of the proudest moments of my life. It signified over two decades of hard work, integrity and a fire in my belly to be the best that I could be. It gave me recognition in a totally different light by the beauty industry and my clients.

There was a time when I used to look at the past winners and nominees of the BABTAC Awards and wonder if I'd ever see my name there. It felt like a dream... one of those sacred goals you hold close, not because you need validation, but because deep down, you know what you're capable of, you just need to prove it to yourself.

I never thought for one moment I would win.

I admired everyone who entered the prestigious BABTAC Awards, they were and still are such inspirations to me, year after year.

Chasing that dream over the years required me to stretch myself in education, experience, business, be industry diverse and hold onto self-belief.

The journey to that stage wasn't always glamorous, as you have read. It was late nights, long days and extended stays away from home. This includes endless learning and being honest with myself about where I needed to grow. Transformation can be very uncomfortable but it's always worth it.

Winning the awards meant that I 'could' win. It changed my inner voice. That was a real moment of realisation and gave me a sense of purpose to guide and support, not just my clients in their own lives but other therapists to realise they too can achieve their ambitions and goals.

I know having won awards, it takes courage, reflection and self-belief to go through the challenging yet positive judging process. Just entering, even if you don't make it through the first time is a powerful and positive energy. If you don't put yourself forward, you will never know how far it will take you.

I remember my first awards night at the Professional Beauty Awards, London. I just sat there at my table most of the evening, dazzled by the lights, drunk in the atmosphere. My eyes wide open and in total disbelief at being surrounded by so much talent. I struggled to truly believe I was there as a finalist. I didn't win that first time, but I felt a winner just being there! (Of course, I did it all over again).

Shine Creates Shine...

Success and knowledge has much more meaning when shared. When you help others rise, you rise too.

My Shine Values Are...

S - Soul-led: Following my intuition and working from the heart.

H - Healing: Through touch, energy, intention and helping others to feel whole.

I - Integrity: Staying true to my values, even when this meant taking the longer path.

N - Nurture: I believe in lifting others, sharing knowledge and mentoring with care.

E - Evolution: I never stop growing, age has no barriers or ceilings.

Every day I am privileged to make people feel better about themselves and see their inner sunshine radiate. Treating their skin is the superficial element, the real confidence and change comes from within. I go home every day knowing I have made someone feel special and worthy. I try empowering people to stand taller in their own confidence to shine outwards from within.

When I think of people who inspire me, they all have a special presence. A calm confidence with an aura that lights up a room. They draw you in and making you feel so welcome and included. They have an ability to show their vulnerability, along with imparting experiences that didn't quite go to plan and sharing how they grew from those challenges.

'Don't shine so others can see you.
Shine so that through you, others can see themselves.'
C.S. Lewis

My mentors always made me see the bigger picture yet encouraged those small and often slow steps on the journey. They helped me see myself differently. Their belief in me made me brave enough to pursue things I might have once talked myself out of. They let me glimpse the map but gave me the compass and reminded me that I knew the way.

I will be forever grateful for their light. My legacy is to help others shine through with intention, consistency, integrity respect and kindness.

'It's never just a facial®…'

About Andrea Simpson

Andrea Simpson is a solopreneur, best-selling author, multi award-winning facialist, international educator and respected Key Opinion Leader with over 25 years in the beauty and wellness industry successfully establishing herself as a leading figure and visionary in the beauty industry.

Renowned for her intuitive, innovative heart-led approach, she blends advanced skin technology with Ayurvedic wisdom with her award-winning Autograph Facials, that have earned her a loyal global following, including royalty, celebrities, and high-profile clients.

'Facialist of the Year' at the BABTAC Awards, Andrea is a featured speaker at Professional Beauty and the founder of The Facial Mentor, inspiring others to pursue their dreams, establishing her as a guiding light for aspiring solopreneurs and skincare therapists alike.

www.andreasimpson.co.uk

www.thefacialmentor.co.uk

Insta: @andreasssimpson_facialist

Insta: @the_facial_mentor

Just A Beauty Therapist

Joanne Serrant

I am just a beauty therapist.

That's how I referred to myself for years, just a beauty therapist, running my little salon. Those words put a lid on my potential, keeping me in a box I didn't even realise I had built for myself. Until one day, someone helped me see things differently.

At 16, I began training in Bradford as a beauty therapist, massage therapist, and reflexologist. It took four years. The dream? Move to London, become a makeup artist, and live that exciting city life. But life had other plans. A few years before college, I lost my little sister to cancer. Watching my family navigate that kind of pain was heartbreaking and it showed me that life can be cruel.

As a teenager, I didn't truly understand the weight of losing Helen. I was surrounded by a loving family and caring friends, but when you don't even realise you're struggling, how can you ask for help? I drifted through college, quietly carrying that heaviness. I enjoyed beauty therapy; it gave me structure and a sense of purpose, but I held back from chasing the bigger dreams, unsure of myself and what I was really capable of.

Then, I found massage. Or massage found me. There was something about it that just clicked. It felt nurturing, intuitive, and natural. I noticed how people softened under my hands, how their energy shifted, and how they left differently than they arrived. I felt an almost spiritual connection. My massage skills were the reason I got my first job, and quickly became the treatment my clients returned for, time and time again. Helping others feel better made me feel better; it gave me a sense of value.

Then, my mum began her battle with the same disease that took my sister. I didn't want to face the reality of what was happening. I made some bad choices throughout her illness, possibly to distract myself, and then... she was gone. My rock, my wise woman, who always knew what to say, when to say it, or when to say nothing at all. I shut down, boxed myself in, made myself small, and played safe. If I stayed inside my little world, maybe nothing else could be taken from me.

One day, a wonderful client noticed my energy, maybe how flat I had become, and invited me for a Reiki treatment. I didn't expect much, and during the session, I didn't feel much. But afterwards? It was like the world had regained its colour. She told me, "You are here to make a difference." I smiled, but inside, I thought, I'm just a beauty therapist. Becoming a Reiki Master set me on a journey to explore energy and spiritual work. As a massage therapist, I had always felt a connection with human energy, but Reiki opened up a whole new perspective; it was different and sometimes unsettling. I wasn't ready for it, or sure how to handle it, so I kept a lid on this too.

Life has a funny way of nudging you in the right direction, even when you don't realise it at the time.

In the early part of my career, I ran a busy, successful salon with my friend Clare. We were doing work we genuinely loved, but didn't fully understand how to be business owners. We often worked 45-plus hours a week, were constantly in demand, but still didn't see our own worth.

Then my husband's job took us south. Away from our friends and family, and away from my business. It was a huge move for us as a family, and we had to start over.

We'd moved to a gorgeous spot in Berkshire, and I stumbled across a house that I instantly decided was ours, then spent a few weeks convincing my husband of the same! During the renovation chaos, I started to see the potential for a home-based business, and once complete, I was ready to get back to work. I kept things small - massage and facials, nothing too 'out there.' I retrained in advanced treatments, followed trends, bought machines, and took every course going. Clients loved the advanced treatments, but it was my massage that truly resonated with them. And yet, at just £45 a session, I was fully booked but struggling financially. But what did I expect? I was just a beauty therapist.

Social media, understandably, gets a bad rep, but for me, it showed me what was possible. I started seeing facialists positioning themselves as experts, sharing their skills, and owning their worth. It was inspiring. I returned to a Signature Facial I'd created years before, a treatment that blended advanced skincare, intuitive touch, and energy work that I loved. I worked hard and took time to refine and perfect it, and it became my most sought-after service.

At the same time, I was working with a wonderful coach who helped me see the stories I had been telling myself: fears of judgment, fears of being seen, and fears of building something that could be taken away. I realised that if I wanted more for my life and my career, I had to step out of my comfort zone. And that terrified me. Deep down, I was afraid of success. I had tied it to exhaustion, judgment, relentless work, and being absent from my children. But facing that fear allowed me to reimagine success in a way that worked for me.

I realised the change had to begin with me! I invested in myself and my business and got the financial advice I needed, began to dig deep and started treating my business like a business. When my not-your-average accountant, Jo, went through my numbers, the reality hit: I was booked solid yet barely making minimum wage. Jo painted a vision of what was possible, but it meant making real changes. And real change is scary.

One day, I broke down while speaking to my brand rep, Julie. I was tired, I'd done the work, right? I had a vision, but how did I move from just a beauty therapist to a successful businesswoman? I wanted more, I could feel it. I knew I was capable of earning more, creating more, giving my family the experiences I dreamed of, and, most importantly, finding the freedom to be more me. She listened, really listened, so as a thank you and Christmas gift, I invited her in for a facial. That single act changed everything. As I worked, she relaxed into the treatment and then said, "Nobody does facials like this, Jo. Have you ever thought about teaching? Think about it." And just like that, a door I hadn't even realised was there opened.

She lit a fire in me. That Christmas, I wrote my first training program. Within a week, 16 clinics expressed interest in working with me. Over the next year, I took my techniques, my passion, and my drive to help others into those clinics and even to spas. To my surprise, I was good at it. The feedback was outstanding. I loved it.

Now, collaboration has always worked well for me; I have not been afraid to invest in myself or my business, and every time I have, I've seen the return. I began to work with an incredible coach who pushed me to dream even bigger. She helped me embrace the spiritual energy and soul work that had always been woven into my treatments and bring it unapologetically into my training and marketing. She saw where I was different and helped me own it. My accountant helped me structure the business so that training could be a core part of it. I had the vision. I had the experience. I had the support. It was time to shine!

Finding my confidence was the biggest challenge. In the early days, I compared myself to other trainers, wondering if I was really adding value. Could I fill the courses? Who even wants to learn from me? But the difference was clear: my flow, my energy, my way of blending intuitive and intentional touch with technique. That was my gift.

Now, I am proud to be a beauty therapist and charge properly for my clinic services. I run booked-out workshops teaching The Art of Intentional Facial Massage. I have an elite online membership. I've spoken on stage, sharing my journey, and hopefully inspiring other therapists to step into their potential. My mission is to light that spark in others, to help them dig deeper, feel more, and craft unforgettable experiences that come from their heart and soul.

Too often, we stay small because we think it's safer. But the truth is, everything truly incredible lies just beyond our comfort zone.

Over the past four years, I've had so many moments where I peeked around the corner and thought, 'That's not available to me', but time and again, I've felt the pull and realised that I am meant to walk this path.

My advice? Surround yourself with people who see your potential and who encourage you to dig deep and face the fears that are holding you back. Because those fears, they're exactly where you need to go to heal and grow. See your future big and bold. I've been blessed with an incredible family and collaborated with powerful women who have inspired, challenged, and shown me what's truly available. My mum, my rock, shows up in so many of these women. I feel her guidance all the time. They've helped me stop being afraid to shine.

And now, I pass that light on to others, through my facial massage, through my training, through every therapist I help step into their power and creativity.

So, stand up. Stand out.

The world is waiting for you to just be you!

About Joanne Serrant

Joanne is a heart-led advanced facialist, trainer, and entrepreneur who helps therapists elevate their treatments and confidence. With years of hands-on experience and a deep passion for her craft, she teaches results-driven facial massage rooted in intentional touch and soulful connection.

After running a successful salon, Joanne founded The Skin&Soul Academy – a space where technique meets intuition.Through workshops, 1:1 training, and masterclasses, she shares a deeper way of working that blends energy work, intuitive flow, and purpose-led practice.

Joanne believes that when therapists embrace their magic, they don't just transform their business – they transform lives. Her mission is to help them reconnect with their power and shine in their own unique way.

When she's not teaching or treating, you'll find Joanne at home in Berkshire with her family, diving into a new course, or dreaming up her next soulful project.

joanne@jsadvancedskincare.co.uk

Instagram: @skinandsoul_academy

https://www.instagram.com/skinandsoul_academy

www.jsadvancedskincare.co.uk-Pro Zone The Skin&Soul Academy

Strange Reactions

Kath Reade

My travel book *Jumping Over My Shadow* was published recently. That in itself was a great thrill, but when it raced to the top of the Amazon charts across the UK, USA, Canada and many other countries I began to feel - well, what did I feel?

When my publisher congratulated me on becoming an international best selling author, I was, for the first time ever, truly speechless.

I had achieved many professional successes to be proud of in the past, but it has been a lifelong dream to have a book published and it came true in my seventy third year on this planet.

There was no doubt, however, something was gnawing at me, and I did not know what.

Friends congratulated me and were surprised at my apparent diffidence. One exhorted me to enjoy the moment, and I heard myself reply "I daren't!"

I expect you are familiar with dancing around with joy, only to have your joy dashed by some disaster or turn of events.

That had happened so often in my life that I was apprehensive in the counting chickens department.

I was almost anticipating being told it was all a complete mistake. Expecting to learn that my book was not successful at all but had been mistaken for someone else's that had flown steeply up the Amazon rankings. Cue the Impostor Syndrome.

It did seem though, that there was no mistake, and my book had not only got to # 1 in the Amazon rankings but was staying there. The delighted chuckles of my excellent publisher continued.

So what on earth was the matter with me? Why was I all at sixes and sevens, unable to wholeheartedly celebrate this achievement? Why was I walking about with narrowed eyes and a 'too good to be true' grimace?

There was a swirling fog of deep emotions somewhere in my being that I could not get a handle on.

I morosely searched Netflix for a film to take my mind off the constant stream of ever more impressive worldwide rankings data sent hourly by my publisher.

A biopic of the life of Beatrix Potter would be just the thing. Pleasantly mischievous rabbits in blue jackets would take my mind off the puzzle of being a globally successful author.

Lo and behold, the film was in fact about the author attempting to get her books published. Her father had always appreciated her stories and paintings when she was a child.

Now, Beatrix Potter was grown up and had attracted the

interest of a publisher. Her father came in and held up her published book of *Peter Rabbit*, beautifully and professionally produced.

He told Beatrix that when she had been a child he had indulged her in her charming paintings and stories, and he had enjoyed them. But he now saw her as a seriously talented published writer of whom he was very proud.

At that I simply burst into tears quite unexpectedly. My husband Paul came over and hugged me. I buried my head in his woolly jumper which became wet with my hot salt tears. I sobbed out these words, "I have so much to thank my father for. It was he who always encouraged me to get as educated as possible, who told me education equals freedom, although he, like many others of his generation, had not had the opportunity for higher education.

He who spent so much time with me when I was small, teaching me about the way nature and science works.

He who stopped a teacher from being mean to me and made her apologise to me without once raising his voice.

He who had saved up his meagre wages along with my mother to buy my first guitar, and he, who after supporting me through college, put up banners in my bedroom after I got my degree, and uniquely, opened a bottle of champagne. Like many working class families in the 1970s mine was the first generation to get a degree."

I was crying because he was no longer there, and I could not tell him about my published book. He and my mother would have absolutely loved it. Seeing me become a successful published author, well that would have really made their day. But they are both long gone.

My publisher touched my heart when he said, "They do see it Kath."

At least now the mystery of my strange reactions to literary success had been solved. Perhaps I can now do what my dear friends recommend, and enjoy the moment and the shine.

I thought of the beloved 14th century Persian poet Hafiz and his perfect words to celebrate my dogged self belief and dedication to complete my book, a feat you can also achieve:

'How did the rose ever open its heart and give to this world all of its beauty? It felt the encouragement of Light against its being; otherwise we all remain too frightened.' -Hafiz -translated by Daniel Ladinsky.

I realised the more confidence we can cultivate in knowing who we authentically are, the more we can shine in all aspects of our lives.

Just while reading this I invite you to let go of every reference in your mind to other people's ideas, theories.

This is an exercise to focus on your own authentic thoughts and insights to build your self confidence and emotional resilience by becoming much more your own person, rather than accept the labels others have put on you.

I commend to you an exercise in self inquiry. You can deeply scan your being to see how much of how you think, what you think you believe, comes from others. Maybe from parents (either taking on their ideas or rebelling vehemently against them.)

Maybe from friends and teachers. Or maybe from the increasingly manic social media. We heard ideas that we liked the sound of and so adopted, as well as picking and mixing from what we have read or seen.

Are these acquired ideas the real you?

We can let some of them dissolve away like taking moss from a beautiful stone. For you are that beautiful precious stone.

We can practice seeing deeply into our essential nature and into the nature of all beings and phenomena through meditation. This personal work can be extremely powerful in liberating our true self and our creativity.

We can begin here, now, to delve into what we ourselves actually think and believe.

We can remember who we actually are.

The aim here is to increase confidence in ourselves, to get more comfortable in who we truly are, and become steadily more our own person.

This is not to become less flexible, or deaf to other people's needs and feelings. This is to get to know what are our boundaries, for our own self-preservation and to survive and thrive, with a measure of joy and happiness.

Then we are no longer a pushover, and so we begin to attract those who do not require us to suppress our needs in favour of theirs. We no longer attract emotional vampires.

We are equal to others in deserving our essential needs to be recognised, understood, and met. We see the difference between people pleasing and genuine service to others.

So it is this questioning for authenticity we engage with. Stripping ourselves down as a technician would a computer to see how we work. Then we begin to evolve our own personal truth. As we engage in this process we finally encounter our true beautiful self, beneath all the emotional scars and self doubt.

There are so many ways we undermine ourselves, as others have taught us to, leading to self criticism as a habit of mind. As a challenge to this mindset, consider the revelation that for the most part we are doing our best. That does not mean we cannot improve and develop, but here I offer you a very powerful meditation to realise you are doing your best:

Sit in an upright position with your hands resting in your lap. Gently close your eyes and let your shoulders go down, soften your eyes and your belly. Let tension dissolve through your arms and legs and flow out through your fingers and toes. Be aware of kindness in your opening heart. Let your eyes soften even more.

Each time you breathe in, think the mantra 'I am doing my best'. Let each out breath become a quiet sigh of relief, a letting go.

After five minutes or more of this breathing mantra, sit quietly and sense the effect for a few minutes.

You may be surprised at the flood of relief and relaxation that this mantra meditation can bring.

Fully arriving into your own being will bring a measure of peace, tranquillity, and happiness to your body, heart, and mind. This can be a beautiful springboard to living your talent, and achieving your aims in life.

Join me on the great adventure of self-compassion for personal freedom. You will harvest all the bounteous fruits of your talents and truly shine from within.

About Kath Reade

A social worker and teacher, and highly respected public sector leader, Kath was latterly Chair of Cumbria & Lancashire NHS Authority, and was awarded Outstanding NHS Chair by the NHS Leadership Academy for her work to tackle health inequalities and her expertise in Governance.

Throughout her life Kath has always been a singer-songwriter and writer as her lifeblood. Now in her 70s, Kath is also a trained sound healer, Qi Gong practitioner, and meditation teacher with a loyal following.

She is an international best selling author and has recorded many well reviewed albums of her songs.

'Kath Reade's voice has the silken quality of Bailey's Irish Cream' - Keely Hodgson of The Purple Room 21/9/24

Kath now runs sought after music, qi gong and meditation retreats in the beautiful Lake District and Yorkshire Dales.

Kath lives in Burnley, Lancashire, in England with her husband Paul who is a retired IT professional and a folk singer.

She has one son, Shaun, who is a musician and IT business owner.

www.kathreade.co.uk

The Circle Of Power

Kay Pennington

Life is not a straight line, and you probably wouldn't be reading this book if you weren't looking for some inspiration.

You cannot buy love.

You cannot buy time.

You cannot buy life.

You cannot buy an insurance policy that protects you from undergoing misfortunes, dissatisfaction, change, grief, loss or trauma but what you can do is unlock your inner strength and resilience to help you manage some of life's circumstances and pressures a little bit easier.

The circumstances I am referring to are the ones that hit you like a ton of bricks and bring you to your knees if you let it. They circumstances are the kind when you wake up one day feeling alone, afraid and like you are the only person in the universe feeling so empty low, sidelined, scared and sick from the shock of events that have happened to you.

My chapter in this book is not a self-help guide or a remedy to success, but it is a testimonial of my own truth and how channelling three characteristics of Resilience have empowered me as a human, dictated my career and resulted in some dramatic life choices.

Although money can't buy resilience it can be educated, and I feel strong about this message hence why I created my business, Resilience and Power, in 2024.

As humans we are naturally gifted with some sensory tools and our own individual set of superpowers to enable us to survive life's challenges.

When I talk about superpowers I am referring to your unique gifts. These gifts are in your personal design, and they amplify you and your being. Your gifts become a second nature skill that flows naturally without you even realising. For example, patience is the ability to wait and take your time, making every tread count, focusing on your own energy in your own time. Whilst the rest of world is pushing and shoving to move as quickly as possible, patience can be a superpower. Patience can be the missing piece in the puzzle. Patience is a great foundation for personal growth, growth in relationships and the pathway to finding inner peace.

Laughter... laughter is also a natural superpower.

The ability to laugh is a powerful tool that not only boosts the immune system but positively affects positive physical and mental health by reducing stress. These tools are often not consciously discovered but by tapping into them as well some of the basic senses we can naturally increase our inner strength and stimulate a positive mindset to grow and achieve our wildest dreams.

I'm a big believer of reflection and I encourage it in my workshops. Reflection doesn't always have to be tasking and deep, it can be done whilst spending time on your own in nature, revisiting a place you haven't been to for a while and writing down your feelings or creating your very own actual timeline by putting pen to paper and drawing out your past of events .

Sight, sounds, tastes, smell, feelings and breathing. These are all natural gifts that most humans in the world are gifted with, but how many times in your day, week, month or sometimes a year do really stop to focus on these gifts that provide so much awareness and wisdom to our life. It doesn't matter wherever you are in the world or wherever you may be? On a bus, in a car park, waiting in a queue or walking down a street? By taking a moment to pause and be attuned with the senses of what you are seeing, hearing and feeling etc can evoke a mindful state of awareness. I begin most of my workshops with this technique to reset the mind and body before the session.

What about facing fear? The feeling of fear is one of the biggest setbacks in life and my advice to anyone feeling fear is to use your experience from your setbacks to fuel your determination to succeed. By this I mean, instead of trying to avoid your fear, lean into it instead and address your circle of power.

The circle of power is a term I often use in my Resilience coaching sessions.

The circle is the imaginary ring you draw around yourself and the power is what only you are in control of. By only focusing on what YOU are in control of simplifies your mindset to focus on what you know you have the power to achieve without relying on anyone else's opinion or behaviour. If you are ever feeling threatened or struggling to continue in a demanding situation, the circle of power is a great technique, and it provides a vehicle to carry on.

During my life I believe the circle of power has always been with me. without me knowing it. The amount of times I have heard comments from other people around me saying things like, "Oh a couldn't do what you do', "There is no way I would want to be bothered putting myself through that", "That would be too much stress for me", "How do you keep coping through that?", "I wish I had the strength to do that..."

Without denying, although I received an element of love in my childhood, I was also subjected to experience extreme grief, loss, separation anxiety and traumatizing experiences from an early age.

At the age of 6, I was forced to get into a car in the middle of the night and say goodbye to one of my parents. I didn't understand what was really happening, I could just see and feel the devastation. They didn't want to go, and they were begging to stay. I felt extreme sickness in stomach, uncontrivable fear and I was forced to tell them I didn't love them anymore and I didn't want to see them again. This was not true as I loved them so much and they were always my hero and my happiness. For all my screaming, crying and scratching on the windows of the backseat of the car, it would not change the situation, and it would not make them come back. I didn't see them for another seven years.

This is where my journey into resilience began.

Following a series of incidents that I saw as a child I was taken into care and lived with another family member until I was 18. I am forever grateful for life's experiences both good and bad but after being raised in very turbulent environment as I grew older and reflected on my past, the only thing I wanted to do was break free and find myself and see what the world was really like.

I was so desperate to grow, desperate to love, desperate to succeed and sometimes when you are in too much of a hurry you can trip yourself up. I have paid the price of rushing in too fast, falling into abusive relationships and being buried 6ft under by them. I have experienced the costs of what it takes to get out of them and the strength it takes to rise beyond them.

There is no footprint or roadmap to success, and I will always continue to say that some of the biggest mistakes I have made have been the key to my success but unless you try you will never know?

Following an upbringing of being raised in detachment, grief and loss, I set myself free (or I thought I did?) with hard work, determination which led to immense success. I have lived in big houses, had high paid salary jobs with annual bonuses. I have been given company cars, glamorous rewards and I have been able to afford expensive holidays, handbags, clothes and other luxuries.

On paper, I was living a perfect life. I was winning awards left right and centre for all my hard work and efforts. I had everything or so that is how it was perceived but the reality was not the case. sometimes the universe can see another way for you, and life has another agenda.

Although I wouldn't class myself as old, I feel I have lived, loved and lost everything on more occasions than one.

Sometimes, the reason for the loss have not been in my control and on another occasions maybe it has? Whatever the reason I have ended up in the swamp I have owned it, allowed myself to sit in it, reflected in it and most of all accepted it and the lessons it has taught me. Each time I have dug deep into the darkest parts of my soul, to draw strength, transform and rebuild a new chapter in life again.

Starting from nothing and rebuilding a future completely on your own is a dark place for anyone to be.

If you want to understand what personal growth is? The only thing you can do in life is to keep going, keep reflecting and keep learning.

'If you don't want to get criticized hide from the world. Be nobody, stand for nothing. Never express yourself. Keep your creativity hidden. But realise, that life lived in fear and anonymity is no life at all. Progress and growth demand bravery. Have courage to be disliked while staying kind. Meet cruelty with grace and stand tall in who you are, no matter the noise.'
Vex King

To summarise my top three characteristics of channelling resilience:

1. Self-Awareness

2. Positive Problem Solving

3. Positive Social support.

Self-Awareness is pivotal to channelling your resilience.

By taking time to discover patterns in your own behaviours and emotions provides you with a clearer sense of who you are and what you need in your life to thrive.

Positive problem solving is having the ability to learn from your setbacks, to reflect on a difficult challenge or situation yet be able to break down a problem by finding what is weakening a situation. Evaluating what needs to change so that you can set new goals. The most effective way to problem solves is to break away from old cycles that are not working.

Positive Social support is surrounding yourself in positive influences both emotionally and practically where you feel you can talk openly, bolster your mood, release anxiety and reduce psychological stress. Growing a network of social support can help control emotions and encourage self-discovery and build resilience.

"I believe that everyone is a marvel character, everyone has a super power, You just have to find yours'

What is stopping you?

About Kay Pennington

Kay Pennington is renowned for her inspirational leadership and resilience coaching. Following 25 years of a highly ambitious and award-winning career in the spa industry, Kay is now the owner and co-founder of Resilience & Power Ltd.

Using positive psychology techniques and scientific insights, Resilience & Power offers a range of workshops and programs for individuals and teams to feel empowered. Through her own success and conquering setbacks in life, Kays's passion and belief is that anyone can draw on personal strengths to unlock doubt to conquer challenges.

With her extensive background and experience, Kay has been highly driven to achieve several globally recognised spa leader awards.

Kay has run in two of the world's most famous marathons and is a trustee for The Made for Life foundation.

Kay is also a brand ambassador for Image Skincare UK and works closely with the teams in the UK to amplify confidence and high performance amongst their salons and spas across the UK.

Instagram @resilience_and_power

LinkedIn - Kay Pennington

kaypenpower@outlook.com

Shine Like You Mean It

Lucy Power

I was born into a necessity to dim my light.

My mother was grieving for the baby she had carried to full term before me, and she was grieving for her dear father, who had died when she was six months pregnant with me. She was lost to grief and everyone around her was careful not to make demands of her at this most difficult time in her life. She was lost to me for the first few years of my life and I believed I knew why. I soaked that into my way of being; I believed that she didn't have time or space to love and parent me, I understood that I was both too much and also not enough and I came to the conclusion early on that I was unloveable. I had so much evidence that this was the case that it became irrefutable in my nervous system, in my thinking, feelings and behaviour - my whole way of being in the world was built around my mother's way of being in her grief and as a response to how, when my brother came along two and a half years later, she was ready to parent, ready to love and chose to do so with him. It was too late for me because my personality had already adapted to the pain of not being loved or chosen.

To me, 'shining like you mean it' means being connected with and inhabiting our radical authenticity. I unlearned and disconnected from mine pretty fast. I learned to pretend; I developed a robust and charming exterior, a mask to shield me from the pain of my 'knowing' that I was unloveable. I developed every defense I possibly could so that I could keep myself safe from the gut-wrenching pain that my mother didn't want me; she was there and I couldn't have her.

The cost of this for me was the attachment trauma caused by being unseen, unknown and unloved by the most important person to me during my formative years. It took a lot of healing for me to shine and this is my story about how I remembered where my own personal light switch was.

I pushed through in life, seeing everything as a 'battle to be won' (my mother's words about me). I was relatively successful and deeply unhappy. I got decent grades at school but it wasn't until I got to university that I began to truly enjoy learning.

I remember the moment when I understood that my childhood had been unusual, difficult and complex: I was walking across the campus with a group of fellow students who were sharing how things were for them at home when they were children. I recall being struck by the excessive levels of safety and continuity in their lives, of love and of home. This was starkly different to the discombobulating and inconsistent landscape of my childhood where my mother was sometimes fun and sometimes very angry and rejecting. She blatantly showed preference for and adoration to my younger brother and we literally moved house every nine to eighteen months necessitating many school moves too. My peers that day spoke of sameness, consistency, security and predictability. They spoke of the safety of familial love and I realised there and then that all of these concepts were unknown to me. This revelation shook me and catalysed the process of drawing my attention to my need to understand and resolve my trauma. I soon forgot this and life continued.

I pushed through regardless, enjoyed a great university education and secured a career as a Social Worker and got into the first important relationship for me which was with a woman, Lisa.

I'd understood that I was a lesbian, which added a further layer of feeling like I didn't belong, when I was around twelve. I told my parents straight away and to my surprise I was told that I was wrong, incorrect and that it was simply a perfectly normal childhood phase. As a point of interest, they also told me this when I informed them of my intention to become a vegetarian. It turned out they were wrong on both counts!

Lisa and I were together for around eight years, I believed we were happy for the most part but in hindsight, I think that neither of us knew what to do with each other when the honeymoon period was over and our intimacy drifted into a warm and dissatisfying friendship. She fell in love with someone else soon after our wedding which was held on our seventh anniversary and as soon as I found out that I was no longer wanted and that my wife had chosen another, I fell into an abyss that I needed help to get out of.

This was the start of my journey towards my ability to shine.

We repeat what we don't repair and what was repeating for me, over and over in ways that felt insignificant and in ways that felt insurmountable, was the inevitable relational dynamic first learned in the early absence of love from my mother and in her choosing my brother while bypassing my needs. We'd become a trifecta of unsatisfactory connection, with me protecting my brother from what I believed was risk from my mother, my brother wanting and rightfully needing his mum with my mother reluctantly and resentfully managing the unhinged presence she perceived me to be.

Carl Jung, the Swiss psychiatrist, psychotherapist, and psychologist said, "until you make the unconscious conscious, it will direct your life and you will call it fate." I decided at this point of my life that it was time to bring my unconscious processes out into the light of myself so that I could access my power to choose which way my life would go from then on.

I entered weekly psychotherapy and learned that I had shut off access to my emotions in early childhood as a way of feeling safe, that I had learned to subjugate my own needs and wants and that I was rushing though life, hell bent on being somewhere my mother could somehow begin to love me.

My life continued on its outwardly successful trajectory and after around five years, I began to feel the fizz of knowing that I could be more truly helpful to people now that I'd learned what a feeling, a boundary and what inner peace was and started to prioritise my own wellbeing.

I began the five year trek of training as a Transactional Analysis Psychotherapist so that I could help others truly and deeply in the way that I had been helped. This led me to working with a whole new psychotherapist for a further ten years, qualifying as a Personal and Business Coach and working into how to integrate the two approaches together to help others in a new way, a truly 360° way and becoming ever more self aware and able to direct my own fate.

From the moment I left my job in 2019 to set up my psychotherapeutic coaching businesses, I began to unapologetically shine. I had moved from being restricted by the scar tissue of the trauma my childhood caused into unashamedly self loving, unreservedly seeking true and real joy and connection and unapologetically expanding my capacity for intimacy, truth, authenticity and success.

I'd found that, as my understanding, self compassion and awareness increased, I was able to make purposefully conscious choices around how I wanted my relationships to be, starting with those with my mother and brother and circling out to my friends and intimate partners. I was able, with much of my trauma understood and resolved, to sift through every connection in my life and decide what I needed and wanted to change if it was to continue. Ultimately, I got to choose what I was no longer available for relationally and this left me enjoying the relationships I wanted because they were all happening in a way I was comfortable with. I recognised that my relational world had been overshadowed by critical and controlling characters in a miserable, repeating drama. Of course, once I could, I chose from a place of the squeaky clean energy of my true self.

My life is now full of warmth, love and connection.

The people I choose to spend time with and the relationships that are most important to me all typically nourish me. I fully know and celebrate that I am deeply lovable and I can barely move for the evidence of this.

And these are the results I offer to people who choose to work with me in my close proximity psychotherapeutic coaching experiences today because we are all capable of moving away from the stranglehold that trauma has on us whether it is our own, generational or systemic.

And I coined the phrase 'radical authenticity' which I define as being the unadulterated light in us all, the part of each of us that shines, the core of the shine and the reason to shine.

I work in a uniquely integrative, trauma informed and responsive way to help others to shine as I do now and it delights me. My brother often says with mock grumpiness that I am 'one of those people who left their job to set up their own business and has never worked for a second since.'

Eric Berne, the father of Transactional Analysis said, "We are born princes and the civilizing process makes us frogs." alluding to the fairy tale, The Princess and The Frog, in which a true love kiss releases the frog from a spell and returns him to his original form, a handsome prince.

My psychotherapeutic coaching does the same, it returns you to who you were born to be. It walks you home to the light of your true form, your unadapted self, your radical authenticity.

In radical authenticity you get to choose to live as the

adapted version of yourself or to peel back the froggy layers that you took on to keep you safe during your own civilisation process and shine like you mean it from your true, raw, real radical authenticity.

We all get to choose. You get to choose to shine like you mean it.

About Lucy Power

Lucy Power is an ICF professional certified Personal and Business Coach. She is also extensively trained and experienced in Transactional Analysis Psychotherapy among other therapeutic approaches and integrates these with her coaching practice.

Following a difficult childhood spent in chaos and overwhelm, Lucy has spent all of her adult life searching for meaning and gathering knowledge about how we operate in our hardest and in our best times. Lucy has studied psychology, psychotherapy, philosophy, business administration and leadership, interpersonal neurobiology and complex trauma. She has a Masters in Social Work and has worked with marginalised people with complex mental health struggles for years.

As well as the The Therapeutic Coaching Academy, Lucy offers exclusive 1:1 Trauma Responsive Psychotherapeutic Coaching to help you to recognise, understand and resolve your early childhood wounds and become successful, free of old repeating patterns, feeling safe whatever happens, healthy, wealthy and joyful as a result.

www.therapeuticcoachingacademy.com

LinkedIn: https://www.linkedin.com/in/iamlucypower/

Instagram: https://www.instagram.com/iamlucypower/

Facebook: https://www.facebook.com/LucyPowerICFCoach

When Life Gives You Trifles

Susanne Webb

The moral of my story:

"If you can't yet do great things, do every small thing in a great way"
Napoleon Hill

And:

"Success is no accident. It is hard work, perseverance, learning, studying, sacrifice and above all love for what you are doing or learning to do."
Pelé

The Trifle of life.

My Beauty Salon Business was very nicely established.

My clients were committed and loyal.

And I knew exactly what I was doing!

Nice and easy, steady as you go …

But that was just it!

Predictability, perhaps with a teensy bit of complacency creeping in around the edges?

Looking back and in the spookiest of ways, life was beginning to resemble my Gran's bowl of homemade Trifle…..

At the bottom was a layer of good quality, up right Sponge Fingers that in my mind stood for my steadfast 30+ years of work and loyal clients.

Those Fingers represented my firm direction forward, my eagerness to learn, listen and to put in place advice that I wholeheartedly believed in.

And as the years have passed, I hope they also represent my ability to accept failures without toppling, to hopefully learn from them, put them to one side and to move on.

So, for Me, this layer and these Sponge Fingers could resemble the very foundation posts in my personal life as well as in my business life..

A solid and sound base from which to weather most storms and whatever life throws at me.

In my imaginary Trifle of Life, the Fruit layer comes next supported by the wobbliness of jelly... the perfect picture of life's journey.

The sharp edges and angles of Fruit mixed with the constant wobble of Jelly represents my many times of uncertainty, unpredictability and business sustainability worries that come flooding in from time to time including those most recent Covid years …..

Surprisingly, for Me, this wobbly layer represents super exciting times.

This should be an awakening and an achieving time in the life of a dedicated business owner or any budding entrepreneur.

I feel that without this layer we wouldn't push ourselves and life's rich rainbow of colours would become dull and unexciting.

It makes me question my business and look at Me, warts 'n' all.

It pushes me to take measured chances as well as be constantly nudged outside of my comfort zone, which I believe is an absolutely essential part of any evolving and successful business.

Then comes the comforting blanket of what I know and absolutely love...

The Custard layer.

This represents for me the lessons, advice and experiences that I have learnt to use along the way and the confidence with which I put them into practice.

Custard could also represent how I naturally envelope my clients in warmth, security, knowledge and trust.

For me the words professionalism, dedication and passion for my chosen career could easily be included in this layer.

The Cream and Sprinkles are the fluffiness and light heartedness that we find in life, together with the sharing and giving to those who may be less fortunate or to those who may need our support and guidance.

This layer is for bringing joy, happiness and understanding to others.

And the Cherry on Top …for ALL that I have learnt from my achievements, successes and also from my failures whether they were big or small!

So that's it …Life is like a Bowl of Trifle.

Well, not exactly but there are definite similarities.

The Unexpected Wobble

Recently, I took the opportunity of challenging myself and believe me, it most certainly was not easy but it was just so worth it in many, many ways.

NB: in essence my job is to successfully and beautifully remove different types of non-cancerous skin blemishes, of varying sizes from the surface of the skin. It is a delicate procedure that requires the utmost concentration, skill as well as years' worth of knowledge.

I confidently yet flippantly applied for a National Award without dreaming or even beginning to imagine that if I was one of the seven National candidates chosen to take part, it would be such an all-consuming undertaking. I cannot begin to explain how difficult this exercise was but if there was one thing that I absolutely did know for sure it was that my competitors were going to be equal to me in my years of experience and also in my super mega drive. The best in the business were certainly going to enter this first of its kind, National Electrologist of the Year race 2025.

I think perhaps that most of the intensity of the challenge was down to Me and my personality because rightly or wrongly, I was brought up to believe that when I do something, in fact anything at all, it has to be to the 100% best of my ability…..this mindset has been both a blessing and a curse throughout my life!

So, I decided to dive straight into the sharp and wobbly layer of Trifle.

The super intense but amazingly exciting layer.

I began by taking what I like to call an unpassionate micro-overview of my business.

And to do this I knew that I had to realistically and without emotion look at Me both inside and out.

The good, the bad, what I believed my strengths and my weaknesses were, what was missing from my assets that would make me a more unique and specialist Salon and what further training I could do to make Me the very Best of the Best.

Honestly, I had to find a way to make the judges choose Me above anyone else (did I mention that I was competitive as well as perhaps a little stubborn)?

So, true to form, I gave it my absolute All.

I worked all day in my Salon and tweaked my budding empire by night (and morning)

For advice I contacted colleagues that I knew and respected and I also reconnected with many who had somehow slipped through my fingers and out of my life over the years.

My dossier of achievements were getting thicker as my additional exam passes came through and my beautiful Salon was a sight to behold… all shiny and new with its sleek, state of the art equipment.

On the one hand I was bursting with pride …but on the other I knew I was a complete and utter nightmare to live with!

Fast forward to the serious business in hand, the final day of reckoning.

The choosing of the best Electrologist in the land began with a thorough and very necessary practical exam. There could be no other way to determine the winner of this prestigious Award other than to be scrutinised and assessed by impartial judges for the best choice of probe and correctly chosen technique, as we worked to remove an unwanted or undesired blemish from the skin of our super brave and moderately willing models.

The word 'blur' comes to mind because by this time a haze of light headedness and illness was washing over me and no matter how hard I tried the carefully chosen unwanted blemish was stubbornly refusing to depart from its secure nestling place and equally traumatised host. Until finally by some miracle upon miracle, I managed to grasp a lifted edge and off it unceremoniously came.

The surgically prepared 'treatment' area was now resembling a non stoppable, blood-soaked battlefield and quite frankly a total disaster zone!

My 30 years of supreme confidence came crashing down around me and my dreams of achieving that coveted award were in pieces. Was this my finest hour? It definitely was not! My head was saying 'get a grip, you can do this' but my heart was saying something along the lines of 'drat'.

However, this day was by no means over because next came a crowded interview room with all seven 'renowned' judges.

Of course, being the forever optimist, I still hoped I could find a way to WOW them, turn things around and proudly present myself as the steadfast and confident candidate that I knew I was.

Sadly, that was not to be. Instead, I do believe that I made lovely new friends in that interview room and those new friends and I plus my brave model and a good few others headed straight to the nearby bar to begin an evening sipping an array of strange and wonderfully coloured cocktails... oh what a day and what a night!

To end or perhaps give a rounded ending to this very true story, I would like to mention that the perfectionist and stubbornness in me to give 100% + at ALL costs gave me the dreaded and really quite horrible shingles virus. And I later discovered that although I had employed the services of a professional to test and certify my trusty Machine, the one that I was using on the day of my exam, unfortunately and for some crazy reason it chose THAT very day to depart this world!

And so, back to my imaginary 'Trifle of Life' and the sharp-edged Fruit supported by the wobbliness of Jelly and all that that layer represents.

For me it shows the wonderful although sometimes excruciating unpredictability of life. I could never have dreamt that after all my hours of thought, research and double/treble checklists that the universe had other plans for me.

But was it worth it?

Without a second of hesitation and without a hint or shadow of a doubt... every single step of the journey that I travelled towards reaching my end presentation and its surprising outcome was to me worth every blister of my shingles, every stretch of my nerve as well as every moment of shock and disappointment when I realised that the trophy celebrating my years of achievement was not going to be mine.

However, had I NOT said a big YES to this rollercoaster of an adventure I have no doubt that my Salon would still be happily bobbing along but 'I' would be dull and unexciting.

I would most certainly have remained blinkered and not been forced to look at Me, my business warts'n'all.

The monetary investment into my business would perhaps have been from a more 'when I need it' perspective rather than a 'this is what I need NOW' view point.

And by saying YES the new friends I have met and past colleagues I have reconnected with along the way would never have happened.

All of the above are amazingly important for the ongoing success of a business but personally and for Me above all else... my imagination had been awakened, my mind has been reopened and because of that I see rainbows of colour and potential everywhere I look.

I am no longer cautious about who I am, what I believe in or the levels of professionalism and integrity that I stand for within my Industry.

This amazing book called SHINE is a wonderful gathering of like minded people with their own true and inspiring stories to tell ....thank you so much for inviting me to join you!

About Susanne Webb

Susanne Webb is an Advanced Aesthetician based in the beautiful county of Kent, England, with over 30 years of experience caring for her loyal clients. Her boutique-style salon offers a warm, personal space where clients feel pampered and relaxed.

Susanne's signature treatment is Advanced Cosmetic Procedures (ACP) – the safe removal of non-cancerous skin blemishes – a specialist service she is deeply passionate about and respected for.

Beyond her salon, Susanne is a proud ambassador for the beauty industry, delivering inspiring, down-to-earth talks to schools and community groups. She recently spoke at Professional Beauty, Glasgow, sharing the rewards of life as a solo entrepreneur.

Her newest passion project? Supporting her local under-14 girls' football club.

Susanne is happily married with a grown-up son and she has two huge dogs that are a constant source of both joy and mud!

susanne.webb24@gmail.com

susanne@theskinblemishremovalclinic.com

www.pinebraebeautysalon.com

www.theskinblemishremovalclinic.co.uk

A Learning Journey – Transforming At 57

Fabienne Guichon Lindholm

After reading this chapter, I assure you that you will know that we gain insights regardless of the outcome in any circumstance. We learn... always.

1. The Moment Of Decision

Sitting on the dirty floor at Caticlan airport in the Philippines, where all flights had been canceled that day across the country, I watched hundreds of people busily running around to try to rebook flights for the next few days, and I just knew.

It had already been a few months since I felt in my gut that things needed to change, but I did not know where to start. All the red flags were there, but I kept ignoring them. I felt like an observer of my own life, as if I were watching a movie about to turn into a negative experience. Although my life was very good and I really had nothing to complain about, was very grateful for all I had, for who I was, and especially for my family.

Still, the feeling would not go away; I knew I was at a fork in the road professionally and personally. I was writing my first book, UNAPOLOGETICALLY BOLD, and I kept hearing the voice in my head, 'Walk the walk, Fabienne. If you do not try, you will never know.' This sentence has always resonated with me when I needed to make decisions; I have the syndrome of the fear of missing out. It is one of my saboteurs, and although it has gotten me into trouble sometimes, it is also a way for me to kick myself in the butt and make decisions. I admit this can be risky, but I have to say I have rarely regretted it.

This would be the time to use my transformation cycle again: Regroup, Relive, and Remotion, just as I had done so many times before. But at 57 years old, was I crazy or what? Starting over again was so scary!

2. The Weight Of Past Failures

I have tried entrepreneurship several times before, but I cannot say it was successful; at least, it didn't last. My first attempt at this was before the birth of my first son. My ex-husband and I had just returned from a six-month trip around the world. I was in my early 30s, and I thought this would be the perfect time to create a spa consulting company and use my experience managing and opening multiple spas in North America to support wellness business owners.

I wanted to do this with someone, so I approached a great friend and mentor to launch this business with me. Although it started well, and we were able to complete some notable projects with Harpo Studios (Oprah Winfrey's production studio) and a few others with hotels and resorts, in the end, the financial burden on our newly formed family was too significant.

Therefore, my partner and I dissolved the business, and I went back to working full-time at a corporation. I never saw that as a failure, but rather as an indication that it wasn't the right time.

My second attempt at entrepreneurship came after the difficult experience of being asked to leave my position as spa director. This time, the business model was a B2C model. It was pretty avant-garde for the time, as it involved skincare masterclasses for consumers, a significant trend today, teaching them how to take care of their skin and choose their products wisely. Again, the start was good, but the 2009 real estate bubble had burst, and the stock market crashed along with my business. It was possibly the most difficult time, as I felt that I had failed twice! Once more, reframing my thoughts and focusing on the future, I was fortunate enough to find a managing director position at a wellness center in Chicago.

Yes, all of this was on my mind when I resigned from my global director position. Indeed, it was scary and full of self-doubt, but I decided to jump without a parachute, using my long-time quote, "If I do not try, I will never know."

3. The Turning Point – Choosing To Try Again

So what was different this time? I was in the midst of changing and transforming my whole life, both personally and professionally. Divorce, selling a house, and moving to another country made me think, "Let's pull the band-aid off all at once." I had reached maturity, and I told myself, "If I do not do this now, when will I?"

Again, my fear of missing out pushed me to make the jump.

Perhaps my mindset was different this time; I had learned a tremendous amount in my corporate jobs and from past businesses. While some perceived my shuttered businesses as failures, I considered them valuable learning experiences, similar to attending a class and finishing a project. Yes, they did cost me time, emotional hardship and money, but I was still standing and moving, learning, and creating a vision of how I wanted to spend the rest of my working life. I knew I did not want to remain in the same environment I was in, and I needed to honor my values and my purpose; I had to walk the walk.

I believe that honoring my values was probably the most significant driver for me. The image of myself and what I wanted to achieve in this world was very clear, and I had only a short amount of time to accomplish it. I trusted my gut and ignored a few red flags. I knew it would be hard work, and I was somewhat naïve about how long it would take to be a reliable business. With my impatient nature, I constantly had to reframe my thoughts. Financial stability is also an essential aspect of living peacefully for me; this time, I considered how I would remove the burden of not having a salary for months. Although I had enough savings, it was still nerve-racking every month. However, my values and inner voice were more powerful.

4. The Transformation Cycle: Regroup, Relive, Remotion

Lead by example, Fabienne... I recall telling myself this, as did a few close friends.

My first book was coming out, and I felt like a hypocrite. I had created the transformation cycle that I had used all my life, mainly in a professional setting, and here I was looking at it from an outsider's perspective and hearing the voice: "It is all here for you!"

To me, the *Regroup* section is the most enjoyable part since it allows us to pause, reassess, and redefine our journey. We draw on our past positive experiences to inspire the courage and desire to do more and serve better. It sharpens our purpose and shapes how we wish to be remembered. I often reflect on how I want to view my life when I'm 90 years old, sitting in a rocking chair by the window of my country home in France, watching the snow fall. It's empowering to realize that you did everything possible to achieve your goals, despite the challenges. I evaluated my strengths, pinpointed where I create value, and recognized what people are willing to pay for that value. The journey started to look like a winding road, but it remained a road nonetheless.

The *Reliving* part can be a bit frustrating because this is where we test what we have in our minds, and it doesn't always turn out as we expected. It's somewhat like creating a new recipe from an old cookbook, but in the end, the modern ingredient we added did not enhance the dish, leaving it rather tasteless. So, we experiment a bit with this and that, learn along the way, revert to previous steps, regroup, and ultimately extract lessons and solutions from our past experiences.

Remotion is the exhilarating feeling experienced for a few hours when you launch and clearly follow your designed strategy. You finally move toward what you envisioned. In remotion, it is important to stay focused but not foolish; following a plan is crucial, but adapting the plan as you progress is even more essential. Being agile- this is a phrase I use frequently- without agility, there is no success, especially in the VUCA (volatility, uncertainty, complexity, and ambiguity) world we live in today.

I have repeatedly used these three processes before, during, and after the launch of REV UP YOUR LIFE. The process began in 2021, and I leapt into the great void in October 2023.

5. The Power Of Resilience And Self-Belief

Another quote I often use for my tribulation and keynotes, training, and workshops is: "Sometimes we win, but most of the time we learn."

The learning mindset is what gives us the courage to continue; growth is in our genes. In his book 'The Biology of Beliefs', Dr. Bruce Lipton states that growth and protection are the two behaviors that come from genes, and everything else we learn. This means we have to build resilience.

Sticking to the path and the road is challenging when all the voices inside our heads and from society tell us to stay in a box. Reframing thoughts to positive visions and using past success as a confidence builder is essential. In my case, I kept thinking of a similar move I had made in the early 90's to consistently say, "Fabienne, you have done this before and been successful; you know what to do."

Fortunately, I also had some great coaches who helped me find the bravery and courage to stay persistent and reminded me that I have all the ingredients; I just needed to rediscover them. Resilience does not mean being strong, not feeling down or emotional, or doing it all alone.

It means going deep inside and using positive memories to reassure ourselves that we can do this. Sometimes, we need help, which is okay.

6. We Either Win Or Learn

Shifting the mindset from failure to learning is challenging. Just as growth is in our genes, so is the instinct for protection; we constantly seek comfort. The feeling of being outside the box makes us feel naked, unprotected, and vulnerable, prompting us to activate our fear to hide behind a shield. Naturally, when memories of failure are triggered by our fear, our learning mindset is challenged. I have found that talking to myself continuously and reframing my thoughts while focusing on my values and purpose helps to change my perspective tremendously.

Everyone deals with these shifts in unique ways, and looking for what these thoughts, activations, and exercises are and how to use them will be a journey of discovery on its own. In my coaching practice, I see so many incredible transformation shifts. It is fantastic to see how the human brain can be so flexible and open to learning more and more and over and over.

The key is to have a plan and a structure while being prepared to step aside and change direction. Assessing risks is also an essential aspect of transformation, change, and learning. As Einstein said, "Failing to plan is planning to fail."

7. The New Beginning

It has been 18 months since the great jump. I now sleep at night without waking up in a full panic, wondering how I will pay my bills and what the best direction for my company is. I no longer have the "what the heck did I do" thoughts!

This was undoubtedly my "Jerry Maguire" moment.

I look back on how much I have learned about myself, being a business owner, and entrepreneur. It is still not a perfect picture and all rosy as we say, but I am on my way there. When people ask me where I am in my process, I say, "The train has left the station. It is not going super fast yet, but we are on our way to increasing the speed very soon." I am learning every day, and it is an incredible feeling. I use my past learning experiences and the experiences of others to forge a strong library of thoughts and activities to move forward.

Learning ignites our natural curiosity, leading us to explore new concepts, ideas, and skills. It is a journey that promises to be both challenging and rewarding, allowing us to grow and develop in ways we might never have imagined. I take immense pride in being a self-made female entrepreneur, a role that embodies resilience and determination.

This entrepreneurial journey fuels my desire to continue learning, push my boundaries, and strive for a more inclusive and diverse world. My commitment to growth not only benefits me personally but also serves my community by embracing their own paths of learning and achievement.

About Fabienne Lindholm

Fabienne is a seasoned global learning and development executive with over thirty years of experience motivating and training teams and individuals. Through her company, Rev Up Your Life, she empowers professionals and organizations to become confident leaders who encourage positive change and transformation.

A highly regarded speaker, facilitator, trainer, and professional coach, she has dedicated her career to enhancing wellness and education around the globe, imparting valuable insights into management styles and personal well-being. In the last decade, she has focused on learning and development in a multicultural environment, training and consulting in over 50 countries.

Author of *UNAPOLOGICALLY BOLD* and co-author of *Leading From The Heart*, Fabienne lives in Belgium and is an avid runner, having completed five marathons.

info@fabiennegl.com

www.fabienneglspeaks.com

www.fabiennegl.com

LinkedIn: fabienne Guichon Lindholm

Instagram: fabienne.g.l

Hair, Heart And Hard Truths:
What Leading A Salon Has Taught Me

Melissa Timperley

I'm Melissa Timperley, a celebrity hairstylist, multi-award-winning salon owner, and founder of Melissa Salons, based in the heart of Manchester city centre. I lead a team that designs beautiful hair for clients – many of whom travel from around the world to visit us. I also educate hairdressers internationally and have created an app to help stylists master the art of precision cutting.

From a young age, I knew I wanted to lead and make a difference in the industry I love. I set out to prove that hairdressing is not a dead-end job – it's a powerful, transformative profession. Hairdressers change lives – not just with their technical skills and creativity, but by building trust and confidence with every client. This industry demands creative artistry, science, and huge amounts of emotional intelligence. I've made it my mission to elevate, celebrate, and lead every step of the way.

Leadership Isn't A Formula

When it comes to leadership, I see two paths. The first involves reading every leadership book you can find, applying the strategies, and perfecting management techniques until they become second nature. The other path involves something deeper: a natural ability to connect, inspire, and make decisions – even when they don't feel easy.

After nine years of running my business, I've learned that you can read every book in the world, but at the end of the day, you either have that leadership spark or you don't. Real leadership is forged in action, not theory.

I've had my fair share of challenges, and while books have offered insight, it's the real-world experiences that have shaped me. Leadership isn't about being perfect or having all the answers. It's about showing up when it counts, staying true to your values, and trusting yourself – and your team – even when things get messy.

Leading From The Heart, Even When It's Tough

One moment in my leadership journey stands out. I've always wanted to create a salon where hairdressers can thrive: earn their best wage, feel part of a supportive team, and have their talents celebrated. But there have been difficult decisions to make to protect that vision.

One such instance involved a team member who had been dishonest about personal circumstances. The fallout affected the salon environment significantly. It was a defining moment for me as a leader. I had to address it head-on, with transparency, honesty, and courage. It wasn't easy, but it was necessary – for the team's trust, the culture, and the future of the business.

When you've been 'burned' and you hit rock bottom mentally and physically as a leader, you start to question everything. In that moment, I reminded myself why I started: to create a place where people grow, feel valued, and do work they love. That mission had to be protected – even if that meant navigating some dark times.

There's always light at the end of the tunnel, if at times it's just a faint glimmer.

People First, Even When It's Hard

Leadership from the heart doesn't mean being a pushover. It means making tough decisions rooted in people and values – not just numbers and profit margins.

It's about creating space for your team, your loved ones, and yourself. Sometimes that means making a decision that goes against short-term business interests but protects your culture, your people, and your peace.

Standing strong, being transparent, and doing what's right (especially when it's hard) is what true leadership is all about.

The Importance Of Adaptability: Leading A New Generation

One of the biggest lessons I've learned is how crucial it is to be adaptable – especially with today's younger generation. Gen Z, in particular, views work through a different lens. They value purpose, flexibility, and work-life balance more than any generation before.

As a forward-thinking leader, I've had to check in regularly with my team: What do they need? What inspires them?

What's stopping them from doing their best work?

Leadership can't be one-size-fits-all anymore. You need to evolve, listen – really listen – and understand what your team values.

In today's world, many young people stay in one role for 4–5 years, always seeking growth and meaning. A Gallup poll showed 60% of Millennials are open to new opportunities, and 21% are likely to leave their jobs within a year. That's a huge shift in workplace cultures – and it's on leaders to respond.

For me, that means leading by example. If I ask my team to go the extra mile, I make sure I'm walking that mile right beside them.

The Power Of Transparency: Sharing The Bigger Picture

I've learned that when you're open and transparent about the "why" behind tasks, people show up differently. When a team member understands how their role contributes to the bigger picture, they don't just do the task – they own it.

It's not about micromanaging. It's about making your team feel part of something bigger than themselves. That sense of purpose creates pride, momentum, and powerful results.

Learning At All Times

No matter how far you go in your career, there's always more to learn. I was on a high when my Creative Director Sara and I won the British Hairdressing Afro Hairdresser

SHINE

of the Year Award in 2023. But shortly after, we received pushback online as two white women winning the title — something we hadn't anticipated.

It was uncomfortable at first, but it became a powerful learning experience. I had to educate myself more deeply about the history, politics, and culture of Black hair. I also gained a stronger understanding of intersectionality in feminism, privilege, and the wider industry landscape.

It would've been easy to dismiss the criticism. But facing it helped me grow - not just as a leader, but as a person.

Growth Mindset Through Competition: The Power Of Putting Yourself Out There

Another way I stay sharp in this industry is by entering competitions. I've taken part in many over the years — and I've been lucky enough to win a lot. However even when you don't win there are opportunities to learn and every single one has helped me grow.

It's never just about the trophy. It's about pushing myself creatively, stepping outside my comfort zone, and staying committed to my craft. Competitions help me benchmark against the best, get inspired, reflect on my own evolution and see what we could be doing better.

There's a vulnerability to putting your work out there and inviting judgment. But that process builds resilience. You learn how to take feedback, how to grow from it, and how to keep going — even when things don't go your way.

More importantly, I show my team what it looks like to go for something wholeheartedly — even without a guarantee of success. That's the mindset I want to instill: courage, creativity, and continuous growth.

Being Kind To Yourself

When you run a business, it's hard to switch off. But I've learned that protecting my time and energy makes me a better leader. I don't work past 9pm, and I keep that time sacred for my husband and myself.

As someone in a physical job, I'm also mindful of my menstrual and hormonal cycle. I shift my routine depending on how I'm feeling, giving myself extra rest or changing up my workouts when needed. These small acts of self-kindness help me show up fully – even when I'm not feeling 100%.

Embrace The 'Little' Things And 'Little' Wins

The small things matter. I often rebrand my to-do list as a 'ta-dah!' list – it helps me celebrate what I've done instead of obsessing over what's left.

I also practice daily gratitude. Some days it's as simple as being thankful for a hot cup of tea, but those moments add up. At our quarterly team meetings, I write handwritten thank-you cards to each team member. These small, consistent acts of kindness create magic – and a culture where people feel seen.

The little things aren't little. They're everything.

The True Measure Of Leadership

At the end of the day, leadership isn't about being the loudest in the room or always having the right answers. It's about showing up for your people. It's about standing strong through hard times. It's about making decisions aligned with your values and vision.

Leading from the heart means being authentic, being brave, and never losing sight of why you started. For me, it's always been about creating a salon where people feel supported, celebrated, and empowered to shine.

If, through this journey, I can inspire even one person to believe in themselves and step into their own greatness, then I know I've done my job.

And that, truly, is what leadership from the heart is all about.

About Melissa Timperley

MelissaTimperleyisamulti-award-winning hairdresser who works with international brands on hair shows and photo shoots. She is owner of Melissa Timperley Salons in Manchester, England, which she opened at age 24. She now leads a team of 16 professionals serving more than 200 clients a week, generating annual sales of £1m+.

The salon has won multiple creative, marketing and client service awards, including Best UK Salon (twice) and Best UK Salon Team (three times), as well as Afro Hairdresser of the Year.

In 2023, she launched MT Masterclass, a subscription-based online Precision Cutting App which has attracted members from all around the world. Alongside salon colleagues, Melissa also runs in-person cutting Masterclasses in the UK.

Melissa is recognised as a strong female entrepreneur and influencer, having finalised for three national female entrepreneur awards. She lives in Manchester with her husband, James, and their sausage dog, Gregg.

Instagram: @melissatimp @melissasalons

LinkedIn: Melissa Timperley

www.melissa-salons.com

melissa@melissa-salons.com

MT Masterclass

Instagram: @mt_masterclass

Tiktok: mt.masterclass

www.mt-masterclass.com

info@mt-masterclass.com

SHINE

Shine Through Competition

Jacqueline O'Sullivan

In my life and career, I have always believed that what we plan in our minds and how we perceive ourselves will manifest itself into our reality and our lives. This all begins with our mindset, attitude and mentality.

Our mental health is a mix of many things, including our thoughts, biology and environment. A big part of this process that we can work on, is our learned behaviour. These habits, which are often picked up without us even realising it from our surroundings and experiences, can have a profound effect on how we act and how we feel overall. They can be learned from an early age and stick with us, moving well into adulthood.

When we face uncertainty or fear, we often call upon this learned behaviour and to what feels familiar and safe, and in doing so we hold onto what we know, which in turn can hold us back from moving forward and stepping out of our comfort zone into the vast sphere of opportunities that are waiting to be embraced. Sometimes we let opportunities for personal growth slip by because we doubt ourselves. When a chance comes up, it's easy to think it's too scary to grasp and we may choose to back off before we've even considered the options that will start us on this new and potentially exciting adventure.

This kind of hesitation is normal, it's just part of being human but today's fast-paced life pushes us to move past feeling stuck and if we don't make an effort to improve our skills, change our mindset, and gain knowledge, we might miss out on some real and fantastic opportunities. Real growth isn't just about learning new skills, it's also about having a mindset that's open to change. A quote from the author and futurist Alvin Toffler back in the 1970s really hits home: "The illiterate of the twenty-first century will not be those who cannot read and write, but those who cannot learn, unlearn, and relearn."

This really speaks to me today, especially since we're in a world that needs us to quickly pick up new skills and forget outdated ways of thinking. Sometimes we may even need to go back and relearn skills or knowledge we may have forgotten. Toffler's words remind me to look at what's stopping me from chasing my dreams and to not fear change, while still being able to use the skills, experience and knowledge I have already gained.

So, what's holding us back? Why do we hesitate when new opportunities arrive? I believe at the heart of this is how we see ourselves and the value we place on our worth and what we have achieved. It's important to take a step back, be proud of what you've achieved and to see the worth of your contributions. When you appreciate yourself, you naturally develop respect and love, both for yourself and others. It's easy to fall into an excuse-making trap and it can become a habit that feels comfortable, yet also limits our potential. We need to recognise when we're falling into that pattern, since it keeps us from exploring future opportunities. Don't fear failure, it's part of the growing process, failure isn't the end, it is an opportunity for learning and a stepping stone to getting better. Our culture can often confuse us with what success means, since it's often connected to status, looks and fame. This can make success seem out of reach for most, who are using these standards as their life compass. If we chase these ideals, we might lose sight of what really matters and end up feeling disappointed.

These unrealistic standards, sometimes called 'perfectionism', can lead to feelings of imposter syndrome, where we feel we must perform perfectly all the time and if we slip up, we worry it will show we are not good enough. This kind of pressure can affect our focus on actual work, keeping us stuck in a cycle of worry. Breaking this cycle is tough, but it starts with remembering that nobody's perfect, and you can only do your best. Imposter syndrome can often make us feel out of place, so it's helpful to remind ourselves of our achievements and that we deserve to be where we are in our careers or lives. It's important sometimes to focus on our own wins instead of comparing ourselves to others. We can strive to become a better person today than we were yesterday.

What I have learned from living with this mindset, is that encouraging my learners to join skills competitions can really help in their development and learner experience. This allows me to pass onto them the skills and knowledge I've gained in over 30 years of teaching and industry experience. This wealth of information and real-time understanding helps them build confidence and resilience. Dealing with challenges and setbacks is a huge part of any skills competition cycle and through these experiences, the competitors learn that perseverance and hard work is crucial to reaching their goals. This resilience isn't just valuable in competitions, it's important in everyday life.

As an educator, these competitions give me a chance to help my learners set realistic goals as I guide them through breaking their objectives into smaller more manageable tasks. The skills they pick up along the way benefit them in competitions as well as in school and life, helping them develop a success-driven mindset. Plus, competitions often mean working with peers, which helps build social skills like teamwork, communication, problem solving and conflict resolution.

The hard work and dedication needed from both educators and learners in these competitive activities highlight commitment and discipline while learning in various settings, not just in the classroom.

The ongoing practice, training and pushing for improvement create a strong work ethic that helps in all areas of life, whether in school or their future careers.

Even though only a few might reach the top tier of success, this shouldn't stop anyone from striving for their full potential. I'm all about encouraging them to grow and shake off limitations. This is their opportunity to learn new skills, expand their knowledge and boost their self-esteem while facing the future with fresh determination, ready to learn, unlearn, relearn and SHINE in everything they do. I have been able to watch my learners grow within a competition cycle, from reading and understanding a brief to creating wonderful pieces of work. The confidence, resilience and maturity that this brings to them never ceases to amaze me and is one of the highlights of my work.

One of my favourite quotes is from Canadian philosopher Matshona Dhliwayo: "Your mind shines brightest when you enlighten others; your heart, when you encourage others; your soul, when you elevate others; and your life, when you empower others."

Helping others reach their goals and discover their potential brings me so much satisfaction and has played a big role in my career success. Being able to make a positive impact on those around me allows me share my passion for personal and professional growth. I aim to inspire others by creating a supportive atmosphere where they feel confident in their actions and skills. I challenge my learners to widen their perspectives and aim high, always valuing their dreams over my own needs. I encourage them to concentrate on their own performance and improvements and not compare themselves to others.

I think it's crucial for my students to feel accepted, even if we don't always see eye-to-eye. I'm here to cheer them on as they find their way, especially during tough times, setbacks or when they feel stuck. I stress that facing and overcoming challenges can boost confidence and sharpen problem-solving skills. I try to create an environment conducive to learning and to ensure the success of my learners, I establish clear boundaries. I believe it's essential that the classroom is a space where learners feel free to express themselves and I impress upon them the importance of leaving any issues they may have at the door.

The relationships I build in the classroom often go beyond just learning as many of my former learners become friends and even come back for mentorship during their careers or when competing. Not all my former learners stay in the industry, many have gone onto higher education or changed careers. However, seeing them succeed and watching some of them thrive in their new chosen fields and lives using some of the skills they developed while with me, fills me with pride and fulfilment that beats any of my own personal achievements. I always share my knowledge and experience with learners and push for them to reach their full potential and in some cases, they have surpassed my own skill levels.

Helping people shine in their lives and careers keeps my own light shining bright and keeps me motivated. I truly believe we owe it to our young people to understand, support and educate them. They're growing up in a world that's so different from the one I knew, and while it's difficult for us to fully grasp their experiences, we can try to understand them and find ways to guide them towards reaching their full potential in this fast-changing digital age.

About Jacqueline O'Sullivan

Jacqueline O'Sullivan is an award-winning educator, including Scratch Stars award winner for 'Services to the nail industry'. She has proven teaching and motivational expertise and a vast experience delivering first-class training and assessments in nail technology, make-up, beauty therapy, customer care, nail art and procedures within pressurised settings. She holds a BA(Hons) Degree in Education and is involved in judging numerous national and international nail competitions including Nailympia and is the competition director for Professional Beauty Magazine Competitions.

She has over 30 years' experience in the nail and beauty industry and has worked with a number of awarding bodies within the further education sector. Jacqueline has also worked with several industry brands throughout her career and helped create private training courses and worked on product development. During her career she has mentored nail artists and beauty specialists to numerous industry competition titles. Jacqueline also sits on the board of directors of HABIA.

jacquionailpro@gmail.com

SHINE

Uncovering The Diamond Beneath The Surface

Diane Hey

Each of us is born with an inner brilliance – an untapped light and power made up of our unique gifts, passions and potential. Like a diamond formed under pressure, we all hold many sides to ourselves, waiting to be discovered, explored, polished and brought to the surface.

But growth, like nature, is not always smooth and certainly not predictable.

Life brings with it storms, and challenges, moments that will test us, which can create a layer dust to cover our natural shine. Setbacks, failures, self-doubt, and disappointments can all dim that brilliance, some people carry those events heavily through life, not realising that underneath it all their potential remains, waiting to emerge, waiting to be polished.

In my own journey, I have faced those same moments – times of doubt, lack of confidence and even imposter syndrome. I've questioned how I found myself in certain roles, leading or achieving things that once felt out of reach. There have been knocks and low points, but I have always held onto optimism and integrity. I have welcomed each challenge as a chance to grow, stretch myself, make things better and embraced the learning it gave me – even when it was uncomfortable. In terms of that learning, I refer to life learning not just educational pathways and this holistic learning is what has helped me to move forward, achieve my goals and find my successes, big and small both personal and professional.

Success isn't a one-size-fits all, we all have a different view of success, and what that looks like to us, different starting points and a varied toolkit shaped by our life experiences. Knocks, setbacks, failures and disappointments... chip away at our confidence, mask our abilities and dim our brilliance. Over time these layers can become heavy, and for some they stay that way – living with a cup half empty view, burdened by doubt, fear and missed opportunities. That's what can sadden me the most when I see untapped brilliance hidden under the layers. I believe growth is about understanding where to start, adding to each person's toolkit, building new skills, attitudes and perspectives that support transformation and progress.

My experience and insight have been gathered over 35 plus years in an industry I love, it is a privilege to Chair various National education standards setting groups and hold strategic roles, also be a business owner, educator running apprenticeships and other regulated pathways to employment and self-development programs, and always keeping my routes as a practitioner in the spa, beauty, health and wellbeing industries. I have been fortunate to support both young people and adults in my career and have made it my mission to help uncover that hidden diamond.

To inspire growth, my aim being to help each individual rediscover their brilliance, develop a mindset that thrives in change, and recognise that, like nature, we are all meant to evolve, and our greatest learnings and strength can come from our hardest challenges.

My Approach: Lighting The Way For Others

Whether someone is at the beginning of their journey or finding their way back, growth happens when we create the right conditions. Here's how I aim to support and nurture that process:

Inspire Growth Through Challenge

Growth doesn't happen in comfort zones and familiarity. I encourage those I work with to lean into the challenges, to step up and to give things a go and risk getting it wrong, or a setback with further work, that's where real development lives. Whether like learners who have dared to dream of accessing their next steps, entry points, interviews, questioning if they have they the right grades, attitudes to convince the interviewer of their abilities, we've explored their fears, planned their pathways and they chose to grow through action, they went for it. That spark of confidence changes everything.

Stay Curious And Honest

Growth is sparked by curiosity, it is not about pretending that everything will always be perfect, it's about showing different ways to see the world and our place in it. I create space for honest conversations and alternative viewpoints. We don't suppress discomfort, or hide from difficult conversations, we talk openly and unpack it. When something doesn't sit right, we talk it through. Because choosing silence or distraction only delays learning.

Take Ownership And Accountability

To enable growth everyone must learn to be accountable, owning their errors and their successes. I help people understand how their decisions influence outcomes and have consequences both negative and positive. With ownership and accountability comes empowerment - the power to shift direction, shape character, and build resilience.

(And yes, sometimes the journey gets intense – but it always comes from a place of belief in what's possible and always real).

Offer Time And Be Present

Growth can't be forced or rushed; we each have a variable capacity and need time to absorb and reflect. I never say, "I don't have time", when asked for support, making time shows care, it tells someone they matter, they are seen, heard and worth the effort. Consistency, patience and being present allow people to feel safe enough to take the risks, lean into the challenges that create change and can be the difference between someone giving up the challenge or giving it their best.

Listen

When we feel truly listened to, we build trust and give space for people to be heard. I create an environment that empowers people to speak, and I respond with encouragement and practical support and techniques. If a strategy doesn't work, we try another, because that's what real growth is, progress, not perfection.

Embrace Learning In Every Moment

Everyday moments hold lessons. Whether someone is quiet or outspoken, fast paced or considered, their efforts must be recognised. Growth isn't about being the best, it's about becoming better than you were yesterday, one step at a time, each to be celebrated!

Reflect And Reframe

Reflection is where growth takes root. I teach people to weigh up decisions, review and assess situations, consider the outcomes and reframe challenges as feedback, with an opportunity to reflect, regroup and improve (grow). Whether a project succeeds or not, they learn to make decisions with clarity and confidence, always offers insights, and those insights build on their resilience.

The Power Of Going Forward
Why Does It Matter So Deeply To Me?

Because I have lived it, and I have seen it time and time again in others. I have watched hesitant, sometimes written off, uncertain individuals evolve into confident, capable people and professionals, who begin to own their space, use their voice and walk in their purpose.

Growth as explored is not just physical, it's emotional, psychological and deeply personal. Like nature we are constantly transforming, shedding what no longer serves us, dusting off any layers that dull our brilliance, pushing us back towards something brighter.

Growth is mindset with adaptability and the energy that

opens the door, allows us to step into the room and start our journey.

Through each challenge, each decision, and each breakthrough we add more tools to our toolkit. Those tools are developed through experience, interactions and saying 'YES' to new things. Every experience adding a new tool to our personal growth toolkit and skills that not only help us navigate life but help us shape it, improve it and celebrate it!

Ultimately, a growth mindset allows us to rediscover the brilliance we were born with and helps others uncover theirs too, standing taller, speaking clearer and with confidence, and when more people rediscover their shine, the whole world becomes a brighter place.

About Diane Hey

Diane Hey, Founder & CEO of Armonia Health and Wellbeing, holds over 35 years' experience in spa and wellbeing industries. She's renowned as an industry expert, and advisor focusing on apprenticeships and professional training in spa, beauty, wellbeing and aesthetics. In 2000, she launched Armonia Health and Wellbeing, including Armonia Training Academy, an Ofsted-rated, Government-approved institution. For over 25 years, Diane has championed employment-ready education, collaborating with various UK Government initiatives and departments to create and uphold standards. As a technical advisor, she works with all UK national educational regulators, holding key advisory roles and chair positions. Diane is dedicated to setting standards, evident in her role as a Trustee for Touch in Cancer Care (SATCC). Additionally, she chairs the National Occupational Standards for Hair and Beauty Industry Authority (Habia) reviews and the BWA apprenticeship trailblazer group, also serving as a BABTAC Board member. Committed to elevating wellness sector standards, Diane focuses on regulated educational pathways, fostering talent pipelines and sustainable career development. Her exceptional contributions were recognized with the Industry Beyond Award in September 2023.

Careers@armonia.co.uk

www.linkedin.com/in/diane-hey-31190583

The Power Of The Superpower

Madeleine Geach

What are your greatest strengths?

I always ask people this question at the start of coaching them. I work with the leaders of some of the best restaurants in the world, and despite their achievements, many of them leave the answer blank, and most of the others stop at a few hesitant words.

And yet not knowing how to answer this question - whether this comes from a fear of sounding cocky or simply having no idea - is our biggest obstacle to growth. And once you figure it out, everything falls into place.

The Power Of Positive Feedback

Most of the people I've coached are ravenous for feedback. And part of my role is to hold up a mirror for them and reveal what they don't see. Because when you own and run a business, there's no one around to give it to you; no boss or peers offering their perspective. You're leading in a vacuum, unaware of your blind spots.

And without this knowledge you cannot grow.

But here's my biggest learning over the years: the powerful breakthroughs don't come from discovering what we're bad at or need to improve. The real eye-opening moments happen when we realise our strengths. We are even more blind to our strengths than our weaknesses. And it often takes someone else to help us truly see ourselves.

I experienced this myself with a former boss. Years ago, he casually mentioned that I was good at bringing structure to things. At the time I shrugged it off. Bringing structure to things felt just like breathing. And I took it for granted. But that one piece of positive feedback changed everything. Slowly, I begun to consciously use my strength and bring it to my work. Once I did this I became more and more successful at what I did. And it nudged me down a path where a decade later I now help founders bring structure to their creative thoughts. Many of my clients have ADHD and/or are highly creative entrepreneur types. The structure I can bring to their thinking is just what they need.

What strengths are you taking for granted?

Your Strengths Are Your Superpowers

Your greatest strengths are your superpowers. Once we recognise our strengths, that's when the magic happens. We start to feel more confident. We take on challenges with a new mindset.

I've seen founders who I work with paralysed by competition. And I'll admit it's a trap I've fallen into myself: those weeks (or months) when it feels like someone else is doing it better, faster, or louder. It's a completely human reaction. By knowing our strengths, we can bypass the competition trap.

Take Elena. When she came to me for coaching, I was immediately struck by her talent. She had built a thriving company from scratch in her 30s and become the go-to person in her area of our industry. But beneath the surface, she was consumed by imposter syndrome and fear of being overtaken by the competition.

I've seen the same issue over and over again for the business owners I work with. This mindset is like a poisonous worm. It eats away at your energy, distracts you from your own work, and convinces you that you're not enough.

The antidote? Knowing your strengths.

Superpowers + Confidence

I sent Elena off to create her own 'brag file'. The name is ironic, tapping into the false belief that knowing our strengths is showing off. It's not! A brag file is a private folder filled with evidence of your wins plus the skills and strengths that made them possible. If you've never done this before, try it. Start with 20 strengths, skills, or achievements. If you're stuck, ask trusted colleagues, mentors, or friends for feedback. Add testimonials, milestones, reviews, kind words from customers or clients - anything that affirms what you bring to the table.

Once Elena knew what her strengths were, her obsessing about the competition faded away. When you see your strengths in black and white, your perspective changes. You stop fearing the competition because you're grounded in who you are and what you do best. You no longer compare apples to oranges - because you understand your own flavour.

Superpowers + Success

Many of us have been taught, often without anyone saying it out loud, that the way to succeed is to be hard on ourselves. That if we just push a bit more, criticise a bit more sharply, we'll finally get it right. That self-doubt is a kind of fuel. But over time, that kind of fuel runs out. And it leaves a bitter aftertaste.

In my world, Michelin starred restaurants, I encounter many top chefs who only know this way of working. They've built their careers in tough environments that demand perfection, where you get better by constantly fixing flaws (in a recipe, in a menu, in yourself) and eradicating them. The trouble is this way can leave us exhausted and unhappy.

When one of my most memorable clients Seb came to work with me, he was heading in this direction. Highly self-critical, on the edge of burnout and depression, in our first session he sat on my sofa and stared into a cup of tea in total despair. He'd built an up-and-coming group of financially successful, well loved and respected places to eat. But in session one he could barely see any of that.

Constantly focussing on his faults had left him worn down. And this resulting low mood and confidence was threatening his business. He was, like many of us, just far too harsh on himself and thought that recognising anything good was arrogant.

There is another way. We begin to thrive not when we ignore our flaws, but when we stop making them the whole story. Knowing your strengths is a more compassionate but also more effective way to succeed.

One that won't wear you down or burn you out.

7 Superpower Habits

If you want to build a deeper connection to your strengths, here are seven habits that will help you own and grow your superpowers:

1. **Ask for positive feedback.** Reach out to friends, mentors, colleagues, or team members and ask: "What do you think I'm really good at?" Listen with curiosity.

2. **Create your Brag File.** Start a digital or physical folder filled with your achievements, praise, and proud moments. Keep adding to it. Review it when you need a boost.

3. **Name your top three superpowers.** Write them down. Say them out loud. Let them anchor your confidence and guide your decisions.

4. **Use your strengths daily.** Ask yourself, "How can I apply one of my superpowers to this task or challenge?" When we use our strengths intentionally, we get better results and more joy.

5. **Spot your strengths in action.** At the end of the day or week, reflect: When did I feel in flow? What was I doing? What strengths was I using?

6. **Celebrate your wins - even the small ones.** Take a moment to acknowledge progress. This reinforces your strengths and builds a habit of recognition.

7. **Pay it forward.** One of the most powerful ways to understand your own strengths is by helping others name theirs. It sharpens your awareness and deepens your insight.

A Final Thought – Paying It Forward

I saw a cheesy quote the other day on Instagram, and it stayed with me. To inspire people don't show them your superpowers. Show them theirs.

Thinking back to my old boss and his feedback all those years ago I now know this to be true. If you notice something good in someone, tell them.

You never know how far it might carry them.

About Madeleine Geach

Madeleine Geach is a Leadership Coach and founder of hospitality coaching company The Good Life. Working with celebrated chefs, top restaurateurs, and leaders of London's most acclaimed restaurants she helps them to create some of the best places to work - as well as eat – in the country.

In recent years she has twice been named one of the Most Influential Women in Hospitality alongside greats like Angela Hartnett and Skye Gyngell (by CODE). She is also a bestselling co-author of the leadership guide *Leading from the Heart*.

Her clients include best in class groups such as Ottolenghi, Hawksmoor and JKS as well as small independents like Rambutan, Elliot's and Trullo. She was previously the Head of Culture at Hawksmoor for many years.

Instagram @thegoodlifecoaching

LinkedIn Madeleine Geach

www.thegoodlifecoaching.net

SHINE

Shining: It's An Inside Job

Anne Taylor

I've just turned 60 years old and am only now truly embracing my light – my shine.

My motto this year? *Love Life.*

As I reflect, the journey to feeling my light and letting myself shine has resembled a hockey stick (I'm Canadian after all, so this is apt descriptor) a gradual incline for the first 40 years, followed by a steep rise over the past two decades, especially the last few years.

In my youth and early adulthood, I often felt something was missing. I grew up in a stoic, traditional family. Emotions were barely acknowledged, let alone discussed. Achievement was the currency of love. I was the reserved, mature, polite child – always trying to please.

Despite a loving home, a long-term relationship starting when I was 18, a university education, and a successful business career, I often felt empty, searching for something I couldn't articulate.

I read every self-help book I could find, had my partner read them too, did all the exercises, attended workshops and retreats, started a gratitude practice, journaled –

and still didn't feel much joy. I didn't really know or appreciate myself.

I was not shining - inside or out.

Everything shifted when my parents died unexpectedly, just 22 weeks apart.

A Pivotal Moment: Loss and Rebirth

Their deaths cracked me open – and *that crack let in the light.*

My Dad technically died from complications of liver cancer surgery. But my belief is he died of a broken heart. He was grieving the slow loss of my Mum to Alzheimer's, the dulling of her shine. Even after surviving colon cancer a few years earlier, I think he simply lost hope. His shine was gone – and then, so was he.

My Mum was diagnosed with lung cancer in the same hospital where my Dad had died two months earlier. How? Months earlier a chest x-ray had been clear. Treatment was not possible due to her Alzheimer's. Almost nine weeks later she was admitted to hospital then moved to palliative care. I believe she knew her beloved home had been sold, and without my Dad, she didn't want to live any longer. She chose her moment to extinguish her light.

My rebirth took much longer.

For about eighteen months, I lived in a fog of denial and busy-ness.

Work became my escape. Living and working in Switzerland made it easier to avoid grief – I was an ocean away from reminders.

By all appearances, I had a wonderful life: marriage, career, travel, social adventures. And yet – I was still empty.

That's when I began the real work.

The transformative work.

Being Broken Open

I started grief therapy. For the first time, I sat with my feelings instead of masking them.

I realized I was deeply unhappy with parts of my life I had never dared to question: a marriage that lacked emotional intimacy and safety, a career that didn't align with my values and a protective armour around myself to not look flawed, be wrong, or disappoint.

Seeing two people I loved draw their last breaths made life feel finite in a way it hadn't before. The emptiness of losing them felt familiar, their physical absence mirrored my internal void.

And – with my parents gone – there was no one left for me to 'disappoint' with my choices.

I had a clean slate.

Over time, I made bold changes:

- After trying to improve our marriage for two more years, I left.

- I retrained as a coach and left my corporate job to start my own coaching practice, focused on leadership, personal impact and growth.

- I moved homes - and even changed countries – to the UK, a country that had chosen me.

(And no, I wouldn't necessarily advise making those three major life changes all at once. Nevertheless, for me? It worked.)

Being broken open was the beginning of my becoming, ultimately helping me shine brighter.

Shining? (Work in Progress)

It's been a twenty-year journey toward self-awareness and self-management.

Those sound like Emotional Intelligence (EQ) buzzwords however, they aren't for me.

This is real life. My life. Me.

It's been me getting clarity on me, of my thoughts, emotions and behaviours, that's self-awareness. So, I can then consciously choose how I want to behave, think, and feel, that's self-management. This helps me engage better with the other two elements of EQ – social awareness (recognizing emotions in others) and social management (handling interactions with others).

Most days, I shine. Some days, I don't... and that's OK.

Some days, I fall back into old patterns, catch myself, choose differently, and shine again.

What helped me gain clarity?

- **Life Mapping:** I wrote a 20-page narrative of my life to trace patterns, beliefs, childhood conditioning – and, most importantly, lessons learned from all that lived experience. With that awareness, I consciously chose what to carry forward. Adopting more of a growth mindset, than fixed.

- **Coach Training:** Becoming a certified professional coach required deep self-work. It illuminated past wounds and mostly helped me articulate future possibilities and actions.

- **Therapy:** Over time, different forms of therapy helped me to understand my past and how it was affecting my present. I learned to feel feelings, not just think thoughts, and to see how I was sometimes getting in my own way.

- **Leadership Development:** Three major leadership courses, with honest 360° feedback - good and bad - further grew my awareness and most importantly taught me self-management - to be more intentional about my impact on myself, others and in the world and to deal with any unintended impact that resulted

What Helps Me Shine Today

- **Supportive People:** I choose to be around those who acknowledge, support, and encourage my light. They believe, as I do, that shining and helping other people shine results in better lives, more fulfilling relationships, happier people and a better world.

- **Reflection and Intention:** Every night, I write down gratitudes, feelings, celebrations, and learnings from the day - and set an intention for the next day.

- **Meaningful Work:** I am privileged to work with clients who bring their goals, courage, vulnerability, trust, and effort into our coaching and training sessions. Being part of their growth journeys - supporting, challenging, inspiring and celebrating them. Acting as both catalyst and safety net as they step into their own light reminds me of the power of belief, action, and shining from within. When one person shines more brightly, it encourages others to do the same.

- **Structure and Planning:** I use my love and skills for structure and planning to prioritize joy, creativity, and connection by using habit trackers and to-do lists. Sounds dull and predictable - for me it's blissful, freeing and allows me to realize what I want.

And I remind myself, shining isn't about perfection. It's about presence (being consciously present in each moment as much as possible).

My Light for This Year

I thought my 50s were great. I'm even more excited about my 60s.

There's a smile on my face and a twinkle in my eye most days because I decide there will be. I smile and talk to strangers often when I'm out and about (said in a Canadian aboot accent). Most smile and answer back. Shining is catching.

Building on my love of structure and planning, I'm embarking on a *60-4-60 quest*: 60 fun activities and adventures with others between my 60th and 61st birthdays. I did **49-4-49** and **50-4-50**, obviously a decade ago, and loved them. This is about fun, joy, light, connection, living fully, shining – feeling and emitting what I want more of in the world.

To live it and model it.

I've already climbed Scafell Pike (England's highest peak); seen a London West End play, with a friend who is soon to celebrate her 60th, which was recommended by three women I respect; and I've completed a 26.2 mile/42.2km walking marathon with two friends, fundraising for the Alzheimer's Society in honour of my Mum. Many more experiences await, 57 in fact.

60-4-60 isn't just about ticking boxes.

It's about fun, joy, connection, living fully – shining - and helping others shine too.

It lights me up.

I'm told it lights others up too.

Shine Now

Don't wait for loss or external circumstances to teach you how to live. Choose to shine now.

Do it proactively, by motivation and choice rather than reactively, by loss and regret.

Shining is an inside job — and the world needs your light.

My Challenge To You

If your life or the life of someone you love ended tomorrow, what would you regret?

If time and money were no object, how would you live? Who would you be? How would you shine?

And more importantly: *What tiny piece of that vision can you live today?*

What legacy do you want to leave?

What would be your own 25-4-25 list for 2025, your 12-4-12 adventure for this year - or whatever your version of this type of quest might be?

How do you bring some of the essence above to your everyday existence?

Take one small step today. A spark.

Create a simple plan for SHINING this week.

Build a habit of shining every day.

If not now - when?

About Anne Taylor

Anne Taylor built a successful international business career before realizing she was chasing achievement without true fulfilment. Today, she's a certified Executive and Leadership Coach (ICF accredited) and the author of the award-winning book; *Soft Skills* **HARD RESULTS**: *A Practical Guide to People Skills for Analytical Leaders*.

Her career spans 25+ years leading teams and building businesses in Fortune 500 companies in Canada and globally, such as P&G and Nestlé. Now she helps high-performing people and teams bridge the gap between technical excellence and people leadership – and shine from the inside out.

In her Shine chapter, Anne shares her journey of loss, rebirth, and conscious choice: from living on autopilot to leading and living intentionally.

In addition to being the Director of Directions Coaching Ltd., Anne coaches for London Business School.

Through coaching, speaking, and writing, she supports leaders to embrace emotional intelligence, impactful leadership and a life that truly lights them up.

Contact me https://directions-coaching.com/contact/

Email: anne@directions-coaching.com

Website *https://directions-coaching.com/*

Book *https://mybook.to/SoftSkillsHardResults*

LinkedIn *https://www.linkedin.com/in/anne-taylor-6b2a831/*

Insta *https://www.instagram.com/annetaylorcoach/*

*49-4-49: https://directions-coaching.com/2015/07/22/
49-4-49-the-full-list/*

*50-4-50: https://directions-coaching.com/2016/05/05/
the-final-50-4-50-list/*

Shining Through Authenticity

Jaimie Sarah

When I first left the corporate world in the summer of 2016 to establish and grow my coaching and consulting brand, Definitely Definitely, I was absolutely convinced that my role was to be perfect.

The perfect coach, the perfect consultant, the perfect business owner, the perfect divine feminine goddess, the perfectly fit yogi, the perfect girlfriend, perfectly responsive to my clients 24/7, and so on.

I had learned many lessons and skills, and achieved a certain level of success in both my career and life at a relatively young age, and I felt a deep and sacred responsibility to pay this forward and help others achieve more success and make fewer mistakes in their lives and careers. I knew that I could have kept climbing the corporate ladder, but my heart didn't want to. It wanted to impact in a different and deeper way.

Stepping away from the security of my stable six-figure corporate job, I felt an intense pressure to not only replicate but to surpass my previous success.

Although I didn't know it yet, my new identity as a business owner was deeply laden with the pressure of perfectionism. To make matters worse, I genuinely believed that potential clients were attracted to me because of how 'perfect' I was appearing. (Oh, hello Ego Matrix!)

This attitude towards perfectionism, however, proved unsustainable. It wasn't possible to be perfect as a business owner, yet even when so-called mistakes provided valuable insights, the sting of imperfection lingered painfully.

At the same time, I became present to a crucial pattern among my clients.

They felt able to easily share their triumphs and wins with me, but more reluctant to reveal their challenges or vulnerabilities. In particular, relating to enhancing and growing their visibility, a core goal I have always helped clients with, that often has uncomfortable and deep feelings attached. I asked myself why this would be, and realised that of course, the truth was standing right in front of me in the mirror.

I only shared the wins and achievements in my online content and client sessions, I avoided the hard parts for fear of being 'negative'. I didn't really share the struggles or moments of doubt, unless they were from many years prior. And this wasn't just preventing my clients from feeling able to share themselves fully with me, it was also preventing my brand from becoming truly magnetic in the way I knew that it could. I was also unintentionally discouraging openness, which I was shocked and saddened to realise.

Added to this, I realised that although I had made a few brave decisions (most notably, moving half way across the world from London to New York, knowing no one, as well as starting my own business, knowing almost no other entrepreneurs), I was still avoiding certain hard things out of fear of not being perfect.

This insight became a turning point, prompting me to reevaluate my mindset and approach completely. I still wanted to be a good example, but this time not from perfectionism, from ego, from avoidance, or from inadvertent 'toxic positivity', but from care. I recognised that vulnerability and acknowledgement of the hard parts was not a weakness but a profound strength capable of creating deeper, more meaningful connections.

So, I set about both embracing and sharing the challenges too, both in my content and client interactions. The lessons, the disappointments, the hurts, the turmoil. The situations where I wasn't in control or couldn't necessarily predict what the outcome would be. This shift initially felt deeply uncomfortable, terrifying even, but the impact was immediate and palpable.

As I started sharing what I call 'the rainbow' (i.e. all colours) of the human experience more openly, my clients and online audience alike responded by mirroring my transparency. They began freely discussing their fears, their feelings of inadequacy and their hidden vulnerabilities, too.

I noticed that my clients began crying more often during sessions, laughing more often, feeling their feelings more often and more fully. I noticed that they felt able to expand differently, not just with me but in their brands and in their content. I also noticed that in my group programs, participants' vulnerability inspired and catalysed other's growth too.

A profound transformation had begun unfolding, characterised by deeper trust, greater emotional depth and more authentic growth. And to my delight, it was rippling outwards!

This new approach was not merely about transparency, but about embracing imperfections and mistakes as part of a richer, more authentic personal and professional identity. It led me to understand that perfectionism, rather than being a badge of honour, as I had thought it was previously, was in fact a constraint that limited growth and creativity. Releasing the burden of perfectionism was allowing me to embrace more uncertainty and risk-taking, areas previously avoided due to fear of failure.

I had finally realised that it was safe for me to be vulnerable. That no one would run away or never want to hire or work with me again if I was vulnerable. I also began to realise that my vulnerability was a true gift to others. That it helped inspire and educate and empower, just as much as when I shared my successes, if not more! I noticed that any sneaky imposter thoughts I had been carrying before, based on the illusion that I must always be perfect in order to be good enough, dissolve in their entirety.

Of course, embodying this shift began to naturally inspire and catalyse the same possibility for my clients too, especially since I was sharing about it openly in my content.

This was both fortunate and timely, not only as it aligned more closely with my brand values, but also because shortly afterwards I became a mother (those of you who are already mothers will know that peace with imperfection is absolutely essential to staying sane as a mother!), and then a single mother by choice.

My newfound willingness to be vulnerable and authentic meant that I was able to not only accept this, but to honour it as an integral part of my story. I was able to be a beacon for other mothers, including unexpectedly single mothers who were struggling with their own fears of imperfection and of failure, and what it meant about their worthiness, both personally and professionally.

Navigating personal uncertainty, I encountered numerous setbacks and moments of genuine struggle. Each of these instances, previously potential sources of shame, became instead opportunities for deeper learning and growth. They reinforced my commitment to authenticity not just as a personal virtue but as a professional strategy capable of profound influence.

I noticed that the more authentically I shared, the more impactful my messages became. It wasn't just that vulnerability invited empathy – it created a safe space for others to express themselves genuinely. My openness encouraged others to explore their own authenticity, inspiring them to embrace their whole selves rather than segmented, polished versions of themselves that weren't truly them. (Which had previously created inner conflict for them too.)

Embracing authenticity and vulnerability not only changed how my audience felt able to express themselves, it also became essential for my emotional wellbeing during this intense life transition. Rather than hiding the difficulties of mostly solo parenting while growing a relatively new business, I openly shared my experiences and lessons, finding strength in the encouragement that emerged around my honesty.

It allowed me to provide authentic leadership grounded in empathy, courage and genuine understanding – qualities far more potent than superficial perfectionism.

Further amplifying my impact, this shift attracted new connections and clients who resonated with my vulnerability. People seeking authenticity gravitated towards me and my work, resulting in more meaningful engagements and collaborations. Those who preferred surface-level interactions naturally drifted away, a process I recognised as both healthy and necessary.

Ultimately, learning to shine through true authenticity reshaped my entire professional and personal narrative. Every single relationship in my life either became deeper, or fell away. It helped me to build profound connections build on trust, mutual respect and authenticity. I witnessed clients achieving unprecedented breakthroughs, inspired by the genuine exchanges we shared.

Through this transformative journey, I've come to an understanding of the value of both vulnerability and authenticity. Authenticity does not mean the absence of excellence; rather, it invites a deeper kind of excellence – one grounded in honesty, openness and genuine human connection.

As I look back, I recognise that my initial aspiration to project perfection was not inherently flawed – it stemmed from a sincere desire to inspire and lead effectively. However, true leadership and impact emerges not from perfection but from relatable, transparent humanity. By fully embracing and sharing my authentic self, I've discovered a more powerful, fulfilling and sustainable way to inspire and support others too.

So, next time you are leading, remember that your authentic vulnerability might just be the very gift that those in front of you are waiting for.

About Jaimie Sarah

Jaimie Sarah is a multiple business owner dedicated to empowering individuals to grow themselves and their brands The Aligned Way®. With extensive experience in marketing, coaching and consulting, Jaimie is renowned for her genuine approach, inspiring thousands to embrace their uniqueness and vulnerability as strength. She passionately believes in building businesses rooted in authenticity, clarity and resilience. Through her workshops, coaching sessions, and speaking engagements, Jaimie Sarah has transformed countless lives, guiding people and brands toward their fullest potential by helping them to shine authentically and intentionally every day.

Website: https://www.jaimiesarah.com

LinkedIn: https://www.linkedin.com/in/jaimiesarah

Instagram: https://www.instagram.com/definitely_definitely

Wired to Shine.
Curiosity, Courage And Growth

Louise Baker

Sam shuddered. The email had come in at 7:30 pm. Her boss *reminding* her that the project she'd promised was due. *Overdue.* And as the sun went down, a familiar feeling washed over her – the flood of thoughts, the pressure, and the buzzing hum of mental static.

Sleep didn't come easy that night. Ideas tumbled inside her head. The project hadn't manifested itself into a completed Word document. The words were not ordered correctly. It was all still somewhere lost in her brain lodged between reality, consciousness, and that place of unconscious creativity.

"How can I get out of this?" she thought.

A message from somewhere made her take a deep breath. Avoidance isn't laziness. It's a survival response.

She remembered a mentor once saying, 'Whenever you perceive a threat, it activates a response.' Threat Anxiety Defence. Fight or flight.

It seems so simple but explains so much. If you are being verbally attack by another person, fight or flight is *triggered.*

And you start engaging in highly critical self-talk.

"It doesn't matter if it's fear or avoidance, it's stopping me shine," thought Sam. "When I'm triggered, I'm not doing what I want in this moment."

Sam took another *deep breath* and started to feel herself *settling*.

Here's The Neuroscience

The *amygdala* – our brain's alarm system – scans for danger – social, emotional, or physical.

When it perceives a threat (like judgment, failure, or high expectations), it activates the stress response. *Adrenaline* flows and the *locus coeruleus* (LC) a small group of neurons in our brainstem, flood the brain with *noradrenaline* and the *neurotransmitter acetylcholine* sharpening focus, but also heightening awareness.

We are all familiar with the stress response. The brain gears up to flee or fight. It's an ancient mechanism.

Tucked near the LC in the brainstem is the *parabrachial complex,* quietly helping to guide breath and emotion. Lower down, the *preBötzinger complex* keeps the rhythm of breathing alive.

When you are *trigger*ed your heart rate increases.

When you regulate your breathing – *slow your breathing down* – especially through the diaphragm – you send signals that start to calm the LC. This stimulates the *vagus nerve,* and invites your whole system back into *steadiness*.

Regulated, you change your state and start to shine, again. Unregulated, and you don't.

Simply: we are motivated to move *away from* whatever we perceive as painful and *towards* what we perceive as pleasurable. Away from. Toward.

When you are under stress – a boss clambering for you to meet a deadline, the inferred criticism, someone you feel is verbally attacking you – all *stressors* – you are motivated to move *away from* that stressor.

Here's The Neuroscience

Our brains are predictive organs. They don't just respond – they *forecast*. When the brain predicts – *anticipates, expects* – failure or discomfort, it uses its efficient wiring to steer us away from conflict... but too, often toward avoidance.

Why? Avoidance requires less energy – glucose – than confrontation. And why waste precious glucose on something uncertain?

But avoidance is not laziness. That's why the struggle is real. The brain is hardwired to keep us safe from threats – real or imagined. It does not factor in quality of life, just preservation. And if you've ever felt judged, or not good enough, or less-than, a triggered brain will remember that, and try to protect you from *feeling* those states... again.

Rarely – under those circumstances – will it use energy to create a proactive response. But a *settling* brain *can* and will create better responses. Once you are in a resourceful state to shine... you *can* create new responses.

You will start to shine.

Sam remembered the poem about a boy who shut a cat inside a cupboard... who then, in his imagination, imagined something terrible. He feared the cat was lost forever... trapped behind the door... *because of him.*

The boy didn't know that the door had been opened and the cat released, but that fear had built itself into something far bigger than the truth.

But then, a giant black cat padded out, whole and alive.

We all do this.

We make something bigger than, worse than, more impossible than... and then react as if it were true.

"Was my boss angry with me?" thought Sam. *"What did she mean? Does she think I am incompetent? Unreliable? What did I make that mean?"*

Sam then realised she was *triggered.* And breathed.

Sam saw it clearly now; how easily we let things, good and bad, get stuck in the 'cupboards' of our minds stopping us. How they grow, take up space, twist into shapes too big to deal with. "Here kitty..." she whispered *inside.* "Out you come."

Shining a light of focus inside.

Sam suddenly remembered a nature documentary where a six foot octopus trapped in a rock pool by the outgoing tide, gracefully explored the rock walls and slipped through an impossibly small hole, returning to the ocean.

Incredibly, all six feet of an intelligent creature compressing itself through a gap no wider than a teacup. Glorious.

The octopus was curious enough… to explore for an opening. Any opening. And smart enough to adapt.

Sam smiled.

Here's The Neuroscience

Octopuses are masters of neurological adaptation – decentralized brains, distributed intelligence in their arms, and an innate drive to explore and survive.

Curiosity is a tool to grow.

Humans? Same deal.

Curiosity opens neural pathways, stimulates *dopamine,* and quiets the amygdala's shrill warning bell. It's not just remarkable, it's biochemical hope. And we all have it.

Curiosity didn't kill the cat and it won't harm you, either. It saved the octopus.

And maybe, curiosity could save Sam too.

By now, Sam had made it to work. She plugged in her computer. Walked to the kitchen. *Smelled* the coffee.

Caffeine would just agitate her. And she felt the familiar resistance rise again.

She left. Escaped. Sam crossed the road to the cafe where the *smell* of croissants whispered freedom and simplicity and a hit of gorgeousness. She didn't want a croissant. She ordered a mint tea with it's enticing minty fragrance.

And as she *held* the tea, something shifted.

A memory of all the projects she had completed. The thousands of hours, hundreds of presentations. The many successes. The sparkle of clarity in others' eyes. Sam breathed. Her breath slowed. The minty aroma and the heat of the smooth cup in her hands grounded her.

Here's The Neuroscience

The neuroscience explains that *smell* activates *olfactory* pathways that connect directly to the *limbic system*, mostly bypassing the *thalamus*.

The thalamus acts as a central relay station for all sensory and motor information, processing and routing signals between the body and the brain's cortex: *except smell*. (It's also involved in regulating sleep, wakefulness, and consciousness.)

Interoception, the *internal sense* of what's going on *inside*, along with warmth, scent, touch, and breath, offers powerful non-verbal cues that can help *re-regulate* the nervous system and, wonderfully, rebuild self-trust. Rapidly, once activated.

Smell speaks straight to the *amygdala*, while *touch* sends messages to the somatosensory areas of the brain. In this context, the message is simple.

Sam whispers again, "I'm okay. I've worked this through, before. I'm safe enough to be here."

Slowing the breathing. The smell of mint tea. The touch of the smooth cup – all working to settle the distress. Simple enough cues... but powerful enough to trigger a more beneficial response: shining.

Shining As A Reflexive Choice

Reflexive choice requires a *conscious* effort to analyse decisions, consider outcomes, and connect these insights to broader ideas or theories. Reflexivity takes this further, challenging us to examine our own values, attitudes, thought processes, and assumptions. And *reappraise* situations we perceive as stressful. And *assess perceived ability to cope*.

Shining by deliberate, conscious choice.

Sam moved. She stretched, feeling settled. She began. But how could she build that reflex? The ability to move forward, not in fight, not in flight, but with focus and presence working it through. That's what lived in the space between fight or flight. As humans we have the capacity to use our brains but our brains still want to *efficiently* do the things they are hardwired to do to keep us safe.

We have to *cultivate* that reflexive ability by *consistent* activity and *focus* to build a new behaviour.

Some have to work harder than others. Normalise that.

WOOP

She remembered a tool. A plan. A name: WOOP.

WOOP is one of those words that feels like it's about action and energy and even though it's spelled differently, it still *sounds* a little like *whoop*, as if you're celebrating a great idea, lighting up your sensory system, and sparking a new neural pathway into life.

It made Sam smile.

Wish. Outcome. Obstacle. Plan. (WOOP)

Developed by psychologists Gabriele Oettingen and Peter Gollwitzer, WOOP is not fluffy. It's rooted in decades of research on self-regulation and proactive change.

She paused.

- **Wish:** I wish I shined consistently.

- **Outcome:** I would feel proud. People would relax around me. I could inspire others.

- **Obstacle:** Fear. Perfectionism. Freezing.

- **Plan:** If I freeze, I breathe. If I panic, I write one line. If in doubt, I remember the mint tea.

Her cell phone battery is flat. In the broken sleep ritual it wasn't plugged in. She found the charger, plugged it in, and waited. As the phone revived – *recharged* – so did she.

She opened her notebook and began to write out her *Wish, Outcome, Obstacle* and *Plan.*

Then, reaching for the recharged phone, dictated her WOOP to her voice recorder app. She then looked at the words. She read them. Again. She learnt them.

Here's The Neuroscience: Repetition Builds New Neural Pathways: Focus Your Brain To Shine

The brain loves repetition. If you want to create change, you need repetition. Not once. Not twice. Again and again until your brain builds the neural pathways you need to move forward... naturally.

There are many ways to do this.

You can use flashcards. Draw it out. Write it down. Speak it aloud. You can see it in your mind's eye, hear it, feel it. You can build a picture, a memory, a roadmap in your brain.

We are not fixed beings. Are brains operate on bundles of electrical activity. What you focus on over and over is what you strengthen. Focus matters. Repetition matters. These are building blocks of your shine couple with your values and your beliefs.

People use affirmations: short, sharp statements of intent that keep the mind aimed forward.

Others close their eyes and imagine the outcome seeing the success, hearing the words, feeling the moment like a rehearsal inside the brain. (By the way you don't have to be like an artist in your head the subtlety of knowing and bringing your knowledge in. A sensory way is good enough.)

This is not magic. This is *neuroplasticity*. This is how you *rewire* your mind.

Some use hypnosis to deepen this process. Others meditate on a solution or outcome until the brain starts to believe it's possible and then begins to make it real.

It doesn't matter which method you choose. What matters is that you do what works *for you*. And repeat.

One way or another, find *your way* to build the new pathways that support the life *you want*.

There is no one way, fortunately, because we are all unique. You just have to have *your plan*.

Glancing up, Sam's eyes caught a woman in the corner of the café, gently turning a piece of jewellery between her fingers – a Tiffany-style starfish, simple and luminous. There was nothing showy about her, only a *quiet composure* that seemed to steady the air around her. Something about her *presence settled* Sam's mind too, as if *calm* could be contagious.

Sunlight poured through the windows, catching the star's curve and brightening the whole room. In that moment, Sam realised, shining wasn't just about crafting perfect work. It was also about the community you shined into, their warmth, their laughter, their reflection of you.

The woman stood, left, and others noticed, too. Their smiles connected. She understood. It was all connected, the work, the presence, the light, the human connection.

Exactly what she needed to finish.

Here's The Neuroscience

The neuroscience behind this moment reminds us that growth isn't a solitary pursuit. Through the simple, rhythmic gesture of the woman turning the starfish, Sam's brain mirrored calmness and presence – a nod to the compelling idea of mirror neurons, suggesting we learn not just by doing, but by witnessing.

Sensory experiences like touch, light, and rhythm slow the brain's oscillations, shifting us from states of threat into states of connection. In these slowed, grounded moments, new neural pathways open.

A growth mindset thrives not only through individual effort, but also through the communities that reflect our potential back to us. To shine is courageous. But courage is contagious, too. As is witnessing others courage.

The Energy To Shine

Shining *does* take energy. It takes focus. And direction. A wish, outcome, honoured obstacles and a plan.

When Sam's phone finally lit up, so did she. She worked. It flowed.

Your brain is beautifully built to keep you where you are. It's efficient. It's predictive. It's protective. *But you can rewire it.* If you want to Shine – more often – then it makes senses to identify what works for you. *You have choices.*

Use curiosity. Use your senses. Use your story. Use WOOP. Use whatever works for you. You can change your state from struggle to shine.

And know that the tension you feel is not personal. It's biological. So sit with it. Speak to it.

Your shine is unique. Shine away.

Sam walked back in to the office. She knew that the meeting to discuss the program was five minutes away the team were gathered in the room. She plugged in her laptop, the display came to light, the sun shone through the window but it couldn't compete with the energy and power of a grounded, knowing Sam. Every face in the room lit up and smiled knowing that what was to follow would be inspiring and unique and full of love.

Sam was Shining.

About Louise Baker

Louise Baker MSc brings a warm, neuroscience-informed approach to mindset, wellbeing, and personal growth. With 40+ years of experience as a therapist and commercial practitioner, she combines scientific insight with deep empathy. Her current work focuses on neuroplasticity and AI with *joinvital.ai*, and delivering *whileiwait.uk* — a programme supporting people facing long waits for diagnoses, scans, or treatments, including those with brain tumours.

Louise understands the emotional toll of uncertainty and uses neuroscience to create practical, accessible tools for resilience. A lifelong learner living with dyslexia, she models the same growth mindset she helps others develop. Clients describe her as both grounding and inspiring, helping them reconnect with inner strength, focus, and the capacity to grow — even in difficult circumstances.

Louise's mission is simple: To help people shine, even through life's hardest moments.

linkedin.com/in/louisebaker

https://www.facebook.com/louisebakeruk

https://www.instagram.com/touch_works

https://joinvital.ai

https://whileiwait.uk

Trust Your Own Judgment

Andrew Priestley

I've just finished lecturing a module on Family Business and Entrepreneurship for a London-based, third year MBA course. I had over 170 students.

As you would expect at university level, the module is underpinned by a range of robust theories. The great thing about the family business module is the challenges facing a family business are highly predictable and well documented. My job was to cover off some relevant theories and demonstrate their efficacy with case studies.

The students had to pick a family business... interview an owner or leader about the challenges they were facing... and then apply relevant theories to 'academically' explain the challenges.

The students had a two-part assessment: an 15-minute oral presentation; and a 2,000 word written assignment. The assessment is not a memory test. It's a test of their ability to think and formulate opinions.

A key outcome was to engage students in class discussions.

Essentially, I would present a case study and questions; and they needed to demonstrate that they can think.

What stunned me was an immediate over reliance on the internet and AI tools to formulate 'the right' opinions. I noticed there was a high emphasis on being 'right'.

If this was just this year, or this class, I'd be worried, but this has been the norm over the five years I've been lecturing at uni.

My modules foster an ability to think... primarily because my assignments always involve students engaging with *real people, real businesses* and *real business problems...*

... and then carefully choosing relevant theories... and justifying why those theories are relevant to the case study they prepared for their assessment.

Importantly, their subject should be able to read their assessment and gain valuable insights about their business.

That's a thinking challenge.

I believe University is the right place and time where you are expected to figure things out for yourself. You're expected to have opinions, challenge ideas, and speak about what matters to you.

When you do that, you shine.

But with the internet and social media, commentaries and opinions are on tap. And because students are allowed to take devices into class and access the internet, when I ask a question... my students will reach for their devices and they will rattle off *the facts*. I agree that takes skill, but they are not being assessed on their ability to locate information.

I understand the pressures an MBA student is under especially in their final year. I get it.

And I understand that my class isn't the only class they are attending. And my students will tell me they are completing seven other assessment pieces apart from mine. So, given that, I get why it's easier to 'search' for a pre-baked answer and use that.

But repeating back what they've just read online doesn't cut it at third year MBA level. High school, maybe.

But once I establish that they can find a relevant theory – and that takes skill – I then ask them to apply that theory to the case study being discussed.

It requires them to trust their own judgment – a skill that will serve them way beyond their time at university.

The Expectation To Speak Up

Let's say I ask a question. Usually I get silence. They hesitate. They are waiting for someone else to go first.

My questions are *not* difficult. But they demand more than regurgitating a theory.

But when NO ONE puts up their hand I will call it for what it is. "So, *no one* has any ideas, whatsoever? Let me check. You are all third year MBA students, right? You're in the right room?"

Universities are designed for discussion, debate, and questioning. It's where new and old ideas get critiqued and tested and where you learn to road test your own thoughts.

And I get it – why rely on your own thinking when you

can just Google an answer and see what the internet says? The problem is, if you don't practice forming your own views early – in my class – you will not pass this module.

I'm not testing you for rote learning and recall.

I use the internet and tools like Chat extensively – as a tool – but I then formulate my own opinions.

There's a downside to over-relying on the internet or Chat especially if it starts and ends with a 'search'. And there's so much information out there that it's overwhelming. And often conflicting.

But when a student rolls with whatever *seems* relevant. That's not thinking – that's laziness. It's outsourcing your brain to the internet. The theory might be bang on target, which is all well and good until we sense check it for meaning.

"What did you just tell me? How does that apply to this case study? Why?"

That requires more than curating information.

Here's why it's important. These are MBA students who are going to be dealing with *real people* and *real challenges*. I want them to *care* about the people in my case studies.

I do!

I did a psychology degree and people hire me for those qualifications. When I give a client information it better be grounded in scientific theory. In substance. But I then have to explain *why* this theory is relevant... to the very real needs of my client.

My clients typically have very expensive challenges. They rely on my input to help them make very complex choices based on solid information, not mere guesswork conjecture.

That's why I want my students to go deeper than theories. That requires them to think. And to care.

When they start to do that they start to shine.

And they *feel* it.

Why Thinking For Yourself Matters

So why should you care about all this? Because the ability to think independently and formulate opinions will help you in literally every part of life.

You'll Actually Develop Self-Confidence

Trusting your own judgment means you don't need to check what others think before forming an opinion. Imagine being able to stand in a room, voice your thoughts, and not worry about what others think or second-guess yourself.

That's power.

You Begin To Make Better Decisions

Life throws curve balls. Whether it's choosing a career path, navigating relationships, or dealing with ethical dilemmas, you need to know how to think through things yourself. If you always rely on others to tell you what's right, you'll struggle when you actually have to make big decisions.

You'll Have More Interesting Conversations

Nobody wants to talk to a human newsfeed. When you develop your own take on things, you contribute something real to conversations. People respect those who have well-thought-out opinions, even if they don't always agree.

You'll Develop Self-Trust

You begin trust your judgment. And the more you trust it, the more you *can* trust it.

How to Start Trusting Your Own Judgment

So, how do you actually do this? Here are a few ways to start thinking for yourself.

1. Pause and Reflect Before You React

Next time you come across a hot topic, resist the urge to immediately agree or disagree.

Ask yourself: What do I actually think about this? Where is this opinion coming from? How does it align with my own values and experiences?

2. Read More (And Not Just What Confirms What You Already Believe)

Instead of relying on quick TikTok explainers or whatever is trending on Twitter, go deeper. Read books, check out opposing viewpoints, and learn how different people approach issues. The more perspectives you expose yourself to, the sharper your thinking becomes.

3. Ask 'Why?' More Often

Whenever you hear something that sounds like a fact, question it. Why do people believe this? Who benefits from this being true? If it's true what makes it true? If its' false what makes it false? Could there be another angle? The more you ask 'why,' the more you'll develop your own perspective.

4. Have Uncomfortable Conversations

If you only talk to people who agree with you, you're not growing. Challenge yourself to have discussions with people who see things differently. It'll force you to articulate your thoughts clearly and might even change your mind on some things. That's a good thing – it means you're growing.

5. Limit Mindless Scrolling

We all do it. You open Instagram or TikTok 'just for a second,' and suddenly an hour's gone by. Social media is great for entertainment, but if it's mindlessly shaping your opinions and beliefs, it's time to take a step back. (The internet is a brilliant tool but algorithms identify your 'search logic' and feed you back more of what you already believe. We saw that in the last US Presidential Election.)

Be intentional about when and why you're using it.

6. Trust Your Own Experiences

Your personal experiences, background, and intuition matter. Don't let someone else's *viral* take make you doubt what you know to be true. Your life gives you a unique perspective – own it.

At the end of the day, thinking for yourself and trusting your own judgment is about realizing that your voice actually does matter.

My students come from all over the world. Quite often they bring their social and cultural norms to the classroom.. For example, initially the female students from certain cultures – intelligent and thoughtful – will defer to the males in the room. They will not offer an opinion unless I ask. After a few lectures, they set aside that reserve.

It's a very real challenge to share their thoughts. Especially even when they're different from the crowd.

I teach that the internet is just a tool. But like any tool, you have to be discerning and in control of how you use it.

The next time you find yourself hesitating to share your opinion, remember: You've got a brain for a reason. Use it. Speak up. Otherwise, you will not cultivate the ability to shine.

Importantly – make time to think for yourself.

That's what I am encouraging my MBA students to do.

It is awkward at first, but its gratifying to see their confidence to engage more deeply steadily developing. The class discussions become more lively. And relevant.

The post-module feedback from the students consistently says they loved the classes because they were *pushed* to think.

And in a round about way, they learn to shine.

About Andrew Priestley

Andrew Priestley is qualified in Industrial and Organisational Psychology, an award-winning seasoned business leadership coach, a respected non executive director for established multi-generational family businesses, a best selling author and an in-demand speaker.

He is committed to coaching leaders to lead 'well above the line'. If you are not sure what that means, then perhaps connect with Andrew.

www.andrewpriestley.com

https://www.linkedin.com/in/andrewpriestley

The Power Of Light Bearers

Jen Buck

I was always a competitive kid. If there was a race to run, a solo to sing, or a team to lead, I was always at the front of the pack, laser-focused on being the winner. That drive undoubtedly came from being the only granddaughter among seven male cousins. I was at the bottom of the pecking order – always the smallest – but determined not to be left behind. Wanting to keep up with all those boys, athletics became a big part of my early years. I was often the fastest and most agile on whatever school field or court stepped onto, likely driven by my need to prove I was good enough.

When I got into high school, I was the only freshman girl selected for the varsity track team. Every senior runner seemed intimidatingly mature and far more athletically talented than I could dream of being.

There was a point in that first season when I became plagued by comparison and discouragement. I remember looking at these older runners as we were setting up at the blocks, already deciding that they would most certainly be faster than me before the gun ever went off. As a sprinter, every millisecond counted, and there was no room for intimidation or self-doubt. Unfortunately, timidity took over, and I became paralyzed with the fear of losing.

Because of that growing panic, I started intentionally false starting. In my 14-year-old mind, I figured it was better to jump the gun with a false start than lose the race in front of everyone. After doing this a few times, the varsity head coach pulled me aside to talk. In a flurry of tears and embarrassment, my trepidation came tumbling out, and my insecurity was on full display. Instead of berating me, he firmly told me I would be foregoing my upcoming Spring Break and would have to meet him on the track every morning to practice together for three hours. The horror of losing out on a week of beach fun was only a fraction of my humiliation compared to being caught acting like a quitter.

Those seven days were brutal. There were hours of running, hours in the starting blocks, and hours with a bungee cord tied around my waist, forcing me to run faster or fall, dragged by the rubber rope pulled to its limit. The drag happened once, and you can bet I wasn't going to let it happen again.

While that Spring Break was torture, something shifted drastically in me. I recognized the power of my own mind and body to perform, but also the undeniable power of being fully believed in by my coach.

The transformation in my abilities was tangible. I was focused. I was confident. I was winning. As a result, I was putting more effort into my practices and pushing myself further than I ever had. Somehow, he had reshaped my entire perspective, and the results were exhilarating. I truly became a different competitor after that focused time with my coach. He had uncovered a champion, and I allowed myself to trust the process implicitly, giving everything I had to my goals and execution.

During our last district track meet of that first season, my coach came running up to me in a panic, saying he needed me to substitute for another runner in a race I had never run. Our star senior runner had injured her ankle while warming up, and we needed the points to place first in our district.

While I was always one to jump in and help, this was a race I knew I couldn't complete, let alone win. I had only ever run the 100 and 200 meters, so the idea of sprinting a full lap in the 400 felt impossible. The physical limitations hit me first, and then the crushing blow of humiliation from not being able to win and contribute points to the team made tears spring to my eyes. I told him I couldn't do it. I begged him to choose someone else. I tried to barter that I still had my best race to run, and we needed those points too. With every rejection, I became frozen like a statue, unable to think clearly or move from that place on the infield.

In my haze of self-doubt and panic, my out-of-body moment was aggressively interrupted by his firm words: "Do you trust me, Buck?"

At that moment, in a fuzzy reality, I slowly nodded my head and wiped my tears. He said he had a plan. "I just need you to run your race, Buck. That's it. Run your 200." He reminded me that I could run a 200-meter race faster than anyone in the district, and I needed to do exactly that in this 400. He then told me to look for him on the inside of the track when I hit the 200-meter point.

I started to reject the idea because I was certain my legs would fall off by 200 meters in the race. "Just look for me at the 200," he said again.

I knew there was absolutely no way I would have any strength to go further, and I couldn't figure out how his plan was going to work. Jogging away from me, he shot over his shoulder with a confident grin, "Trust me, Buck – 200!"

As I was readying myself in the blocks for that dreaded 400-meter dash, I remember looking down at my trembling hands as I tried to steady myself on the chalk track. Every alarm bell was ringing, and I knew I couldn't do it. Before I could settle my mind and nerves, the gun went off – BAM! I exploded out of the blocks and told myself to just run my race, moving ahead of every other runner as I ripped through the turn and flew down the straightaway. Approaching the end of the 200 meters, far ahead of my competitors, I frantically searched the inside of the track for my coach, knowing this was when I'd run out of gas and start to sputter. Glancing and panicking, I spotted him, and he was surrounded by about 20 of my teammates. To my surprise, they all screamed at the top of their lungs, "NOW BUCK!" which practically made me jump out of my skin. I felt a wave of power and endurance from that astounding scream, which propelled me forward, maintaining my lead for another 100 meters.

As I rounded the final curve, leading into the last straightaway, I knew I was done. Every ounce of energy had drained from my body, and I was certain that I would spontaneously combust before I could finish the last 100 meters. At the very moment when I was about to give in to pain and failure, my coach and all of the kids were there again, screaming even louder this time, from that final corner, "NOW BUCK!" they roared in a unified chorus. I remember the utter disbelief, followed by a boost of insane adrenaline, as if I had been injected with a superpower.

My entire body came alive. My arms pumped harder and faster than I had ever pushed them. My legs sped up and kept perfect time with the unrelenting driving force of my arms. My lungs, which had been burning and convincing me that I should quit, were suddenly expanding and fueling my supercharged body. My brain suddenly shifted into a space of undeniable ownership and a tangible knowing that I was going to win this race.

And I did. Against all odds, I won that race.

Crossing the finish line in first place, I was flocked by all those screaming kids, crushing me with their excitement. My coach's simple words of 'trust me' and his idea to tap into my spirit, mind, and body were the winning strategy that propelled me to achieve more than I had ever believed was possible.

To this day, I owe that moment to him. To THEM. I didn't win the race because of my talent or mindset. I didn't win the race because I had put in the hours and trained for that moment. I didn't win because I wanted to − I would've eaten bugs to get out of that race. I won simply because others believed in me more than I believed in myself.

The gift of that massive Jedi Mind Trick gave me that win. They did that. Throughout my running career, I've had about a hundred different coaches, and I've been in probably a thousand races from elementary school through college, and I can promise you that there is only one race I remember... *this one.*

That singular moment has shaped everything about who I've become. I look at that race as a distinct marker in time. I deeply understood how important it was to trust the belief that others had in me, and then use that fuel to propel me further.

While I had always been a very social and outgoing kid, it was because of that magical race that I purposefully became everyone else's light bearer. I knew the power of that belief, and I wanted everyone to have that same experience. From that race on, I was at every starting line, pouring my belief into my teammates and racing to every finish line to celebrate their efforts – and I doubled my energies after this moment. Lifting, inspiring, motivating, and believing became my calling card. When awards came around, I received 'Most Inspirational' for the first three years of my participation on the team.

Fast forward to the first day of track practice in my senior year. Full of confidence, I marched up to the head coach to let him know that I was gunning for MVP this year, not Most Inspirational. I let him know that 'I work too hard to only get Most Inspirational.' He didn't take kindly to that, and I was disciplined by being forced to run laps alone for the rest of practice.

That year, after an incredible season, it was time for the awards ceremony. I had high hopes that I was finally getting my MVP.

As the coach started introducing the recipient for the Most Inspirational award, he told the story about the first day of track practice, which got everyone in the audience laughing. I sank in my seat out of embarrassment and sadness, knowing that I wasn't going to get my MVP.

All the work I had done and all of the commitment I had made were being undermined again, I thought to myself. Then he said to the crowd, "Here's what this player didn't understand – the Most Valuable Player on any team is always the Most Inspirational Player. A team cannot function without the inspiration and belief of their teammates, and this person embodies that. So, for the first time, we're giving both the Most Inspirational award and the MVP award to the same person."

And, I got it.

I mean, I really, really got it. I truly understood the bigger picture of what my coach was saying at that awards dinner. For so many years, I was rewarded for being my authentic, enthusiastic self, but somehow I had diminished it because it didn't have the shiny title of MVP.

From that moment on, I used that superpower of authentic inspiration as my hallmark. When we can share our belief, use our inspiration to lift others, and increase the collective energy through positive reinforcement, everything changes. Attitudes and outcomes are transformed because one person makes the choice to shine their light in a darkened space. Be that person – share your shine – the world needs the light bearers.

About Jen Buck

Jen Buck is an award-winning Keynote Speaker who has been speaking professionally around the world for over 25 years. She's spoken at over 10,000 events, in front of audiences up to 25,000 attendees, impacting over a million people throughout her tenure as a Speaker. Awarded one of the Top 100 Speakers To Watch in 2024 and 2025, she is making a massive impact on top leaders in business. Ms. Buck began the first decade of her career in a startup helping to launch a billion-dollar, global and award-winning brand as an Employee Development Trainer.

As a leader, Jen Buck's track record speaks for itself. She's been a Chief Operating Officer, Chief Communications Officer, four-time Bestselling Author with nine books, a Nonprofit Founder, former Chief of Staff for three US Congressional campaigns, and currently leading 30,000 people. Jen Buck isn't just talking about leadership from stages, she's doing it every day.

Website: https://www.jenbuckspeaks.com

LinkedIn: www.linkedin.com/in/jenbuckspeaks

YouTube: https://youtube.com/c/JenBuckSpeaks

Instagram: https://www.instagram.com/jenbuckspeaks/

Facebook: https://www.facebook.com/JenBuckSpeaks

Printed in Great Britain
by Amazon